HARDCORE
REDEMPTION-IN-LAW

Commercial Freedom & Release

Maine-Patriot.com
3 Linnell Circle
Brunswick, Maine 04011

maine-patriot.com

HARDCORE
REDEMPTION-IN-LAW
Commercial Freedom & Release

Contents

Introduction:
The World Of Commerce & The
Courts ----------------------------------- 7
1 In The Beginning You Were Born ------- 17
2 A New Testament Flood -------------------- 25
3 Debtors, Creditors & Redemption ------ 33
4 Loyal To The Crown ----------------------- 39
5 Your Name Is Your Bond ------------------- 43
6 Registration & Redemption --------------- 53
7 Administrative Law ------------------------ 59
8 Ye Shall Be As Gods ------------------------ 65
9 The Obligation Of Contracts -------------- 69
10 Why The Redemption Process Works 75
11 The Commercial System ------------------- 85
12 Subjects Of The Crown --------------------- 95
13 The New World Order Or Release ----- 99
14 Regain Your Standing In Law ------------103
15 On Condition Of Proof Of Claim -------117

16 Redemption Is The Lord's Release --- 119
17 Know Then Who You Are ------------------ 127
18 Come Out Of Her My People ------------ 131
19 Public? Or Private! ------------------------ 135
20 American Bar Association Control ------ 139
21 Esquires - And Who Really Won
        The War --------------------------------- 147
22 The War Of 1812 ---------------------------- 155
23 Treason By Design ------------------------- 163
24 Democracy - *de facto* Or *de jur* --------- 178
25 The 14th Amendment Of Today --------- 191
26 The Privy Token And You ------------------ 202
27 Hidden Tyranny After 1910 --------------- 205
28 The Mark, The Name, The Number ---- 207
29 The Endtime Beast ------------------------- 217
30 The Matrix ------------------------------------ 219

HARDCORE REDEMPTION-IN-LAW

"Ye shall know the truth, and the truth shall make you free." — *John 8:32.*

6 HARDCORE REDEMPTION-IN-LAW

Introduction
The World of Commerce & The Courts

Many are appalled about what they see happening in America today. We are told that America is the Land of Laws; a nation built on law. As a point of fact, nothing could be further from the truth. America is run by people who are lawless.

We have no law in America today; and we need to understand that fact. The law is whatever the Powers-That-Be happen to say it is today; and it may change tomorrow.

So what you need to understand is that America is not a nation of laws, it's a nation of lawlessness. And somewhere along the line we're going to be dealt with by that Universal Law-force some people call God . . . because of what we have allowed to happen in our country over the past 50-60 or so years.

Let us give you a couple of examples of where we think you need to start your thinking.

If you are going to send a package through the mail and you need to wrap it with some rope, you find some rope and tie-up the package, and that should be sufficient for the mailing. But if you're going to take that rope out over the edge of a 10 story building and hang on it, you had better trust and examine the integrity of that rope, now, because you're life will hang in the balance on it.

Another example is if you owned a 2 story building, and you're going to put a lot of weight on the 2nd floor, if you were smart, you would go downstairs first, get up on a ladder near the ceiling and examine the floor above you, that you're going to put that weight on, to see if the floor is going to hold that kind of weight.

What you are doing is, you're standing under the foundation that you're going to build on. You're *standing under* . . . to get understanding, because that's where the word "understand" comes from — to *stand under* the foundation you are building on.

Understanding words is what you really need to begin to do. You need to do your homework and better understand words. If you put an 's' in front of the word, "words", you get "swords", and that's what words are. They are cutting. They can cause you great trouble if you don't know what certain words really mean.

Human beings are word controlled creatures. So we need to establish what words really mean. Again, when we talk about law, there's a Roman maxim in law that says, *"For he who would be deceived, let him!"*

Simply meaning, if you're so unaware as to be deceived, then that's your business. That's your problem, not mine, *unless you ask.* So you need to find out what words really mean. Especially in relation to government and law, because the ancient world of occultism is operating throughout the world today in which you use words; and when certain words are used in a court of law, they don't mean the same thing that you think they mean at all.

In understanding law and the words of law, there are two things that this planet has. Water and Earth. Water and Land. So consequently, *there are two kinds of law.*

The Law of the Land. And the Law of Water.

You've heard of the term Law of the Land, and that's precisely what this word means, Law of the Land, because it is the law of the people who live on the land as *opposed* to something else, the Law of the high seas; the Law of Water. You need to understand the difference.

The Law of the Land is the law of the Culture that lives on the land. So consequently, the Law of the Land is different in every Country. You can do things in America that you can't do in Russia. You can do things in Africa that you can't do in England. So the Law of the Land is the law of the *Culture* that lives on that part of the land.

Humanly speaking, there is a *higher law* that dominates the world. It's called the Law of Water or the *law of the high seas.* The Law of Water is referred to as the *law of money.* It doesn't matter what color you are, or where you're from, or where you live — *money is money.*

And any time you're doing banking, or using money, you are now under the Law of Water — Admiralty Maritime law (AM).

If you go back in ancient history where all of this began . . . back to the land of Canaan . . . the Canaanites were Phoenician . . . *of the Phoenician blood line* . . . and back then, *in the ancient Phoenician language,* 'cana' meant merchant banker. The very word merchant comes from 'mer,' for the sea, or water, as in mermaid, we have the word merchant; merchant bankers.

Let us give you an example between the Law of Water and the Law of the Land. The Law of Water, as I said, is the *law of banking . . . of money,* as opposed to the *law of the customs of the people,* or the Law of the Land.

The Statue of Liberty had to be put on water. It could not be put on American land, as such. It had to be put in the New York harbor, because it is *NOT* the Statue of Freedom, it's a Statute of Liberty.

Liberty is what a Sailor gets when he pulls into port on a ship, he gets liberty. He is not free; he must return to the ship after his liberty. So, America is *NOT* the Land of the Free and the Home of the Brave.

Americans are *NOT* free and Americans are *NOT* brave — *PERIOD!*

We're *NOT* free; America is *NOT* a free country!

Now let me give you an example of how this Law of Water works in the water works we live in. Why is it that you might sometime have to go to court? People are often concerned about going to court.

You go to court, because you play basketball and tennis on a court. How do you play tennis on a court? You play with a Racket. Why? Because that is what court is, it's a Racket.

And make no mistake, they do not pick words by chance.

These words are very serious. They do not use words and terms to no avail. These words are very important.

When you go into a court, what's the idea of going to court? It's a game, like basketball. The whole idea in a court is to *put the ball back into the other guys' court.*

One team gets up, and they throw the ball over to the other lawyer team's court. And that team gets up and throws the ball back into the opponents' court. Consequently, it's a ball game. And the judge is wearing a *black robe,* so he's the referee. The judge is the referee; he doesn't care which side loses or wins because *he's* gong to get paid for what he does *anyway.* So he couldn't care less about who loses or wins the game. He's merely there as a referee. That's why he wears a black robe; *black attire (and that's another subject for another day).*

The judge is a referee between the two teams.

The judge, we are told, rules from the bench. The word bench, in Latin, is a bank. Therefore, the judge rules for the bank.

Where do we find banks? You find banks on both sides of a river. They're called river banks. And what does a river bank do? It directs the flow of the current-*cy* . . . the money. Consequently, your money is currency because it's the flow of cash, the cash-flow.

Let me give you another example of how this works.

When a ship pulls into a harbor, all ships are referred to as female. Air ships, rocket ships, sailing ships, are always female. Why? There's a very good reason.

Admiralty Maritime banking law says that all ships are female because they're carrying items. They're carrying items for money, so, consequently, they're under Admiralty Maritime law (AM). Admiralty is where we get the word Admiral, Admiral of the Navy.

When a ship pulls into harbor it parks at the dock and ties up at the dock. The Captain has to provide a Certificate of Manifest to the Port Authorities because yesterday the ship was not here; but this morning, the ship pulled in, so it is manifested.

So consequently, all the products, $800 million dollars worth of TV's, or Toyota's, or what have you, have manifested. And each one of those items coming off that ship has come off of water, and they have arrived in a ship.

And on a ship . . . all ships have a Captain. The word captain comes from a Latin word, capital; money. So the Captain represents the money that's on board the ship. And, as said before, the Captain has to present the Port Authorities with a Certificate of Manifest for each and every item on board. How much it weighs, what color is it, how many doors it has, etc. So the Captain presents a Certificate of Manifest to the Port Authorities.

The ship is sitting in its berth. The place where a ship sits, when it is docked, is called its berth. She sits in her berth, the berth of the ship.

Consequently, all the items, as said before, came in on water. Each item is an Admiralty Maritime product. And this is true all over the world.

Now when you were born, your mother's water broke. And when your mother's water broke, you came forth, and this is why you have to have a birth certificate, because you are an Admiralty Maritime product under international law, that has manifested.

You are . . . your body . . . is considered to be an Admiralty Maritime product. Your mother delivered you. This is why, if you go to Sears and buy a new refrigerator, they will ship it to you, or deliver it. And that's where you were in the delivery room. Your mother was delivering a Maritime Admiralty product. You came down your mother's birth canal after her water broke.

And as you're taking one of the TV's off the ship, if it falls down and breaks, that's OK — sometimes there are stillbirths, and consequently, you've lost money on that one.

Therefore you have to have a death certificate, and its always signed by the "doc" (doc-tor). The "doc" had to sign your birth certificate and some doc will have to sign your death certificate. All of these words and terms are Admiralty Maritime banking words. Therefore, if you understand lawyers, and judges, and courts, and government; they're all under *international* Admiralty Maritime law.

All religions . . . All churches in the world operate under Admiralty Maritime law. This is why all churches are divided into denominations — like 20's and 50's and 100's. SERIOUSLY! This is why they are called denominations because all churches are nothing more than *products* of Admiralty Maritime banking law.

It's an extraordinary story of occult treason . . . high treason and crimes against the state.

Make no mistake about it. There has never been a court on the face of the earth as far back in history as you can go . . . *there has never existed a country in which the people rose up and demanded their right to be free* — until 1776! The concept of human, spiritual, intellectual, and physical freedom, is a concept that never existed on the earth — before 1776!

The only time that concept has ever come into existence was in the founding of this country, where it was understood that we are Sovereigns who own our bodies — but since 1868 we are now under Admiralty Maritime law.

Think about this . . . about Cowboy and Indian movies where the cowboys would ride into town. They'd get off their horses, *and they were wearing guns.* How come they could walk into a bar carrying guns? And if two guys got into an argument, they could go out onto the street and draw on each other, *in front of the sheriff's office,* and the sheriff would do nothing. How come? How come men could go out onto the street and shoot at each other in front of everyone, *and nothing would be done about it?*

The reason why is this, before 1868, all Americans were considered to be Sovereigns on the land. And one of the nice things about being a Sovereign on the land, is that *you have the right to rule yourself.*

And you need to understand that fact in this last point we're going to make.

In 1868 a corporation was founded. Anyone can incorporate a company in America today.

Well, a company was incorporated in 1868, and in that particular company, the founders of the company called it . . . they referred to it as the United States (corporation), and they stipulated that anybody who wanted to be a member of that company, or work for that company would be called (*not an employee*) a citizen. So today, if you are asked if you are a citizen of the United States, you think you're being asked, *"Are you lawfully in this country to do business?"*

That's *not* what your being *legally* asked at all. They didn't ask you if you were in America *legally,* they asked you a specific question, *"Are you of your own volition, out of your own mouth, testifying that you are a 'citizen-employee' of the corporate United States,"* because in that way citizen of the United States means that you are an **employee** *of a foreign corporation* operating under *international* Admiralty Maritime law.

So today the President of the United States is the President of a *privately owned company.* The company is called the United States, Inc. and the word "president" is a word used in corporate law.

Banks have presidents. All companies have presidents. And so there's a corporation called United States that is *privately owned,* and it has a President.

President Obama is *not* the President of America. President Obama is the President of a *privately owned company;* privately owned out of England.

So you need to understand words and terms.

We believe that there is a divine Presence in the universe, that some men call God, and one day that divine Presence is going to move on the earth, and we're going to see *true freedom* come back to this world. And when it does, you're going to need to understand words and terms, and how they have been used to trick and enslave you today.

HARDCORE REDEMPTION-IN-LAW

1
In The Beginning You Were Born

"Cujusque rei potissima pars principium est" — *"The principal part of everything is in the beginning."*

When you were born, the state became the recipient of your future energy output via your birth certificate as a security title document which the state converted into a bond to be sold on the open market to finance the government's day to day expenses and the interest on the national debt. The holder of that birth-certificate bond is the secured party (*the purchaser*) who is entitled to receive all the benefits of your future energy-output. That energy is measured in money-credits, federal reserve notes (FRNs).

The bondholder owns essentially the results of everything you do. Each person has a *mirror entity* that represents this energy output — his *"nom de guerre"* or *"strawman."* If a *Redemptor* (*a redeemed John Doe*) gets a court summons addressed to JOHN DOE, he can refuse that summons because his name is not spelled with all capital letters and the summons is addressed to his *"strawman"* not to him.

"JOHN DOE" is different from "John Doe."

JOHN DOE is not you, he is your mirror image; your *strawman* devised and set up by government to represent your energy output. Every man, woman, and child has a *strawman.* When you sign your name to any document, you are co-signing for your *strawman* and putting *his property* into the hands of the United States government and its *bond* owners (*stockholders*) — not into *your own hands.* *Your* hands are not really your hands at all, they are *your strawman's* hands.

Commercial *Redemption-in-Law* — a.k.a. the *Commercial Process of Redemption (CPR)* — gives you a way to use this *ruse* to your advantage by taking control of your strawman. Once you control him, you then control the rights and titles to the property that your strawman acquires and owns, and a whole lot more.

The government has *title* to your strawman by presumption only, and if you rebut the government's presumption, you *dissolve* the presumption and gain *title* to your strawman; to yourself. You become a *sovereign citizen* who then holds property, and the government no longer has a commercial hold on you. In so doing you gain *"standing at law."*

Sovereign citizens have absolute mastery over all their property, including freedom from laws, taxes, regulations, ordinances and zoning restrictions. Sovereign citizens are not citizens of the United States government but are *non-resident aliens* (*"denizens"*) with respect to that illegal corporation. The only court that can have jurisdiction over *sovereign denizens* — to try them for any matter — is a *common law court* and such courts no longer exist. *Sovereign denizens* can never be arrested or tried for any crime or matter in which there is no complaining victim. They have various other benefits to boot.

All of a court's arguments are brought to bear against your strawman, which is presumed by the state to be *acting in your behalf.* Because you do not know it and do not rebut their presumptive claim, their presumptive claim is held as *truth in commerce* under commercial law. All failures of patriots in court are thus explained, because they were not familiar with the *"doctrine of the strawman"* and did not have control of their's. They did not *rebut the error* and *declare the truth.*

How do you take back your strawman?

There is a *private side* and a *public side* to government. The value of your birth certificate is posted on the *public, debtor side* of a *double-entry-ledger,* and you need to move this value onto the *private, creditor side* because this side has priority under *military martial law.*

You can take back your strawman by filing your birth certificate and a Bill of Exchange with the Secretary of Treasury, and a *UCC Financing Statement* and a *Private Security Agreement* with the Secretary of State of your state, or any other state that will accept it or in which you can file it. This redeems you, the living soul, from the *public debtor side* of the government and places you on the *private creditor side* instead, after which you have the right of *real property ownership* through your strawman, who now is employed by you the living soul, *as your private employee.*

Not only do you now own directly what your strawman owns, *rather than the State,* but you are now the employer of your strawman himself and his name. Your name is now *your* credit instead of *their's.* If any person uses your name or your strawman's name *without your permission, after you have warned them not to,* they violate the laws of **slander of credit** and this constitutes a federal securities violation.

In essence, your *strawman* becomes a *banker* because it is attempting to collect the security interest underlying your *birth certificate — your contract of presumption with the government of the United States.* A banker has the authority and capacity to create a Bill of Exchange to draw upon the public debt, made payable to the **creditor** of your strawman who is now **you.**

In 1936 your birth certificate bond was given a value of $630,000 and now it is thought to be valued at at least $1,000,000 dollars in real credit. Once you have redeemed your strawman, you can then use *the commercial process* to "discharge" *public debts* with *private credits* in a *tax exempt* and *levy exempt* mode by accessing a private *Treasury Direct Account* (*TDA*) charged against your birth certificate, that you can then utilize to *discharge* various *public debts* . . . but not to make purchases.

When you become the *"holder in due course"* of your strawman you become *his creditor* and the U.S. government, not you, becomes responsible for any claims made against him. If your strawman gets a traffic ticket, you can *have the government pay the fine,* since the government is now the *responsible surety* for your strawman instead of you, and the government is now liable for all public debts, fines and judgments incurred in your strawman's name.

Simply *"Accept for Value"* any *presentment* (*solicitation*) made against your strawman. By this action you are notifying the presenter that *he owes you* the amount of his claim, since you now hold the *true and legal title to the money* the presenter has *offered to you* (as your *strawman's creditor*) in presenting a charge against your strawman.

However, the presenter cannot *turn over to you* (*release*) legal title to these *"public funds,"* because there are none; *the public side is bankrupt and owns nothing by legal title.* This is the advantage that you can use to your benefit. If the presenter does not *produce title* to these funds within 72 hours (*which he cannot do because there is no title*), or withdraw his charge against your *strawman,* a condition of "*dishonor*" occurs and you can do a *Banker's Acceptance* of the dishonored contract. As a private bank you can create a *Bill of Exchange* and deposit it with the U.S. Secretary of the Treasury — now considered to be represented by the IRS.

The IRS becomes the *correspondent bank* of your private *Treasury Direct Account* and keeps an account balance in your name. Once the IRS has established a private TDA for you, you can command the IRS to *release* the *private side funds* (*credit*) from your private Treasury Direct Account to meet *public claims* presented to your strawman. You do this with an *"Acceptance for Value"* credit release and a *promissory note* made payable to the U.S. Treasury and sent to the IRS.

In this way you are given the opportunity to *"discharge"* any *public liability* that your strawman might incur.

In order for you to redeem your strawman, you must follow certain steps, and the first of these involves a UCC-1 filing. You must *register your strawman* with your Secretary of State or with any other Secretary of State that will accept it . . . if your's won't . . . and with your *County Recorder* as well. Secretaries of State are centralized *repositories* for these corporate filings.

The UCC Financing Statement

The debtor and the secured party are listed on this UCC -1 Form. This form shows that a debtor owes money to a creditor — *that your strawman* owes money *to you,* the flesh and blood person.

When debt is charged against your strawman you can *discharge* the debt charge through the *Bankers' Acceptance Process* and the debt no longer exists.

In other words:

When the liability for the debt is charged to your straw-man you can *"Accept it for [its] Value"* and cancel your liability concerning the debt through the *Bankers' Acceptance Process.*

The debt and its liability exists no more. That part of the National Debt is thereby *discharged* and the National Debt is thereby reduced.

This process is called *"Acceptance for Value"* — and the Commercial Process of Redemption (CPR) is referred to as the *"Acceptance for Value" process.*

You can *"Accept for Value"* any *public charge* or *claim* that is presented to your strawman — a traffic ticket, a court summons, an IRS claim, etc. Place a *credit value* upon the document equal to the charge and *command the IRS* to adjust your *private Treasury Direct Account,* accordingly.

In Summation

Who is the *full caps person* JOHN J. SMITH? He is the *legal fiction* that the government created to take the place of the *real being,* John James Smith.

The government has *subverted your birthright* — *your lawful Christian name* — by the *legal fiction* (*your straw-man*) that it devised to take your place in commerce. If the *lawful Christian* answers as the *legal person* the two are recognized *as one person.* But if the *lawful Christian* chooses to *claim his lawful rights* and take control of his government created strawman, the two are no longer the *same person* but are *separated,* and the *lawful Christian name is redeemed.* Herein lies the REMEDY to the entire matter of ***"separation of strawman and state"*** — the lawful Christian no longer allows the government to control his strawman *as a legal person.*

How did this happen?

As part of the reorganization of the United States under Chapter 11 Bankruptcy in 1933, the federal government created a **legal-fiction-person** (*corporation*) called *"The United States."*

Legal fictions can create *legal fictions* (*corporations, fictional "persons"*). So the federal government created other *fictional persons* to represent each one of the several states, *named after each state.* Once this was done, the entire process was set in place — the *"Abomination of desolation"* mentioned in the Bible.

All areas of government, including courts of purported law, are currently authorized by and operating as *fictional persons.*

For example, the U.S. District Court of Western North Carolina can only recognize other **legal-fiction-persons.** This is why your *lawful name* is never entered in their court records. It has been substituted by the **legal-fiction-person** written with all caps. Jurisdiction in such **legal, fiction courts** is only with *other* **legal-fiction-person.** The only jurisdiction a lawful being can enter into is *a lawful, constitutional court* — a *Common-Law, venue* — *but lawful constitutional courts no longer exist. Only legal unlawful private courts are available in America today.*

The purpose and reason for the government's use of *proper names written in full caps* is now revealed.

The only way to *counter this system* of deception is for *lawful beings* to stop responding for the substituted **legal-fiction-names** that the state has given to their strawman.

Every document issued by the government is addressed

to the *strawman person written in all caps.*

Lawful Americans must insist that *they are not the legal fiction* that the government says that they are, and take control of the *legal fiction* (their strawman) by *commercially redeeming and using their lawful Christian name.*

By joining together on the local level each community can begin to *"come out of"* the government's legal, *but unlawful* scheme.

We've all been duped by *"laws that are; but never were."* The government's use of *all caps* in writing *proper names* is no mistake.

"Come out of her, my people, that ye be not partakers of her sins, and that ye receive not of her plagues." — *Revelation 18:4.*

2
A New Testament Flood

"The heavens declare the glory of God; and the firmament sheweth his handywork." — Psalm 19:1.

God is the origin of all law. All of nature testifies to God and to His glory, and Hebrew poetry witnesses to a New Testament flood — *a mirror image of the flood of Old Testament fame.*

In the allegory at the time of Creation, God created His world, *and it was good.* He established Paradise as the Garden of Eden. There he placed Adam and Eve, whom he created, *and they were good.* But after they fell away from God's grace, man became so depraved that a great flood covered the earth and destroyed everyone except Noah and his family *who followed God's Law.*

God put them into a *vessel* called an *Ark.* They had no *remedy* or *recourse* via the *law of the land.* They were converted into *maritime sailors* who survived by the *law of the sea* — until God gave them land again *on which to live.*

A Scriptural *time-of-completion* is **seven years.** And to God each year is as a thousand years. Thus to God a *time-of-completion* is **seven thousand years,** which seven thousandth year has started just about now.

At the *time-of-completion — according to the book of Revelation* — God's people will again be established in a New Jerusalem — a New Garden of Eden — where God's Creation will again reflect the harmony of heaven.

Interestingly, the world has been in a condition of *maritime, admiralty law* now for the past several hundred years. The world is in a *state of democracy* — not a *republic*. Politics is a *world of water* (*a water world*) not a *world of the land*. There is no REMEDY as in the *law of the land*. We are experiencing *The New Testament Flood*.

God has once again placed a *covering of water* over the land *"as the waters cover the sea"* — at a time in history that mirrors and parallels the Old Testament flood. *The first flood* was *physical*, but *this present flood* is *mental — and legal — and spiritual. But . . .*

"The weapons or our warfare are not carnal, but mighty through God to the pulling down of strong holds; Casting down imaginations, and every high thing that exalteth itself against the knowledge of God, and bringing into captivity every thought to the obedience of Christ." — *2nd Corinthians 10:4, 5.*

Man is now on the threshold of a New Era — of a New Beginning. And the prophesy of Thomas More's poetic vision is becoming realized at last:

When from the lips of truth one mighty breath
Shall, like a whirlwind, scatter to the breeze
The whole dark pile of human mockeries,
Then shall the reign of Mind commence on earth,
And starting fresh, as from a second birth,
Man in the sunshine of the world's new spring,
Shall walk transparent like some holy thing.

Has God sent an Ark to save His overcomers today as He saved Noah and Noah's family of the past?

Yes! God established a flood over the *New Testament law-form* to mirror the *Old Testament flood* and to *conceal His plan of salvation* from those who have eyes but cannot see who are not living under the knowledge of His Law. *He did this to give man a time to reign on earth, and "to show you things which must shortly come to pass."*

Your *strawman* is a legal fiction, a *vessel* afloat on the *surging sea of commerce.* This *vessel,* like Noah's Ark, can be the *means to your salvation,* or if you choose not to take command of it, *a vessel to Babylon,* and the destruction that will come *when Babylon goes down,* as foretold in Christ's Revelation to Saint John.

Everyone needs a *vessel* to navigate this *New Testament flood.* The only question is whether you *choose* a vessel under *your control* (*under your own title*) or a vessel controlled by the *kings of this world* (*Babylon*), by surrendering *your vessel's title* (*the title to your strawman*) to a public registrar.

You need your *strawman/vessel* to conduct business on the *surging sea of commerce.* To *separate yourself from your strawman* is to *drown in the commercial sea,* and to destroy your REMEDY at hand.

The answer is not to *separate yourself from your strawman* any more than you would separate yourself from your body. The answer is to *register your vessel* in the *private domain,* instead of *pledging your vessel/strawman to the bankrupt public domain.*

There is no *law of the land* anymore. The world as we

know it today is an *admiralty, emergency, military government, democracy-run, public institution.*

There is no *national sovereignty* anymore. All nations of the world are bankrupt. They operate as *emergency governments.* All emergency governments are *military governments* that control *all public corporations and institutions directly.* Military governments control *private entities* by *contract agreements* and *treaty agreements* between the parties. *There is no law of the land.*

The Constitution of the United States declares that there shall be *no standing Army during times of peace.* But it does not prohibit a *standing Navy* because the *Navy sails the high seas and does not come inland* — in theory, that is. However, the *standing Navy* is being used to subvert the peaceful existence of the people of the land.

There is no land today, so the *Navy sails wherever it will.* The government is in a *state of military emergency.* During war there is no law. There is *no law to protect the people, except their private right to contract* — *to come out of the public domain.*

The Commercial Process of Redemption is based upon the *principles of contract law. It has nothing to do with constitutional law.* It is founded on the concept that *all men have an equal capacity to contract* — unless they surrender that capacity and *choose to be the voluntary servant of a master instead.*

The Commercial Process of Redemption (CPR) is founded on the *concept of **the Pledge*** in which one has the right to *privately pledge one's energy, ones labor and assets, to the private good* — instead of *to the public domain.* It is based in part on the principle that *after one has made a pledge or pawn,* he can change his mind at any time and for any reason, and *redeem that pledge or pawn* — either directly or by way of his next of kin.

We've been made *servants* and *slaves to the world* without our knowledge or consent, and *slaves have no remedies and no rights.* We cannot become *sovereign or free* in our private rights until we have *redeemed our right to contract* through the process of *Redemption-in-Law.* This requires the *paying off* (*discharging*) *the debt* into which we have fallen that makes us debtors to the state. As long as we owe that debt to the state we have no REMEDY and we cannot be free. *But that debt has been prepaid by Christ, Truth.*

We live in a *water world.*

The Navy has surveyed the lands of North America. The surveys were done by the U.S. Coast and Geodetic Survey teams that are a part of the Navy and Coast Guard. The datum point for *survey-elevations* is the *top of the highest peak in the land,* where every elevation below that *top of the highest peak in the land* is deemed to be *"below sea level."*

The world is a metaphorical *ocean of commerce* with no *law of the land.*

No one can carry out *legal commerce* except from the *deck of a corporate vessel.* Scripture talks about *one's body being one's vessel.* Your *corporate strawman* — created in an All-capital-letter name upon its *berth* (*birth*) — became the *name of the vessel upon which you carry out commerce* during the time of your life here on earth. Your *strawman's name* is the name of *your vessel in commerce.* It's the *trade-name* under which you trade.

The military democracy, being an *admiralty, emergency government,* cannot recognize any *real person* in commerce. It only *sees* (*recognizes*) *your vessel* as a publicly registered corporation to be dealt with in commerce under the *law of the flag* and the *registration of the vessel.*

If your *vessel* (*strawman*) is registered *publicly* to the *United States military democracy,* by the application for a birth certificate, your vessel comes under the *laws of the District of Columbia* — *laws of the federal zone.* Your *vessel* meets the conditions and requirements of the *14th Amendment to the Constitution* that was adopted in 1868 (the year of the *Communist Manifesto*). The *14th Amendment* reads: ***"All persons born or naturalized in the United States, and subject to the jurisdiction thereof*** (instead of the Constitution for the United States of America of 1787)***, are 'citizens of the United States*** (read servants and voluntary slaves to the debts of the emergency bankrupt democracy) ***and of the State wherein they reside."***

It is the *public registration of the vessel,* by the application of the birth certificate, that makes one *"subject to the jurisdiction"* of *the United States democracy,* in contradistinction to *the United States republic.*

Your REMEDY is to register your vessel in the *private domain,* instead of to the *public domain that it's now registered to* — to have your vessel *privately controlled, by you* instead of *publicly controlled by the State* — the bankrupt public United States.

Take note of the laws of the *military war zone:* Any vessel sighted upon the high seas *during times of emergency or war* is subject to *inspection, search and seizure* if the vessel *is not properly registered* or if its actions *are not "neutral"* with respect to the warring states.

A vessel *without a flag showing the colors of its registry* is deemed to be *a pirate vessel operating outside the laws of the high seas* and can be dealt with according to the *principles of war dealing with an enemy vessel.* The flag of the vessel is supported by the *registry documents of the vessel.*

The process of Redemption-in-Law is the process of *redeeming the registry of the vessel (the strawman)* from *the public domain,* and making it *private.* And — as in any process of redemption — *there is a debt to be paid* associated with *the pledge and registry on the public side.*

This debt is paid when you *surrender your birth certificate* and *tender a Bill-of-Exchange* to the *Secretary of Treasury of the United States, in his private capacity, via the IRS,* to discharge your strawman's debt to the public domain. Without a *discharge of the debt* there can be no *Redemption of the pawn* — the item pledged — *your vessel/strawman.*

When *the debt has been discharged* you are no longer *a debtor to the state;* you are *a creditor of the state,* instead; y*ou now have standing in law.*

If you have not redeemed your strawman, then you have not redeemed your *vessel of commerce on the high seas.* If your strawman is still owned by *the public United States,* then you — the living breathing soul — are floating in a vessel of the *bankrupt, corporate United States democracy* and *subject to all the laws and privileges thereof.*

The bankruptcy and takeover of the United States did not *destroy the Republic* known as the *United States of America.* The *Republic is still here.* It's just not *accessible by anyone on the bankrupt public side* because *it is private.* You can access it by *your right of private contract*

— *through the Redemption-in-Law process* — IF YOU KNOW HOW.

"For the earth shall be full of the knowledge of the Lord, as the waters cover the sea." — *Isaiah 11:9.*

3
Debtors, Creditors & Redemption

"Judge not according to the appearance, but judge righteous judgment." — *John 7:24.*

Everything you deal with in life has a *reality world* in which you live and a *man-made world* that parallels it in mirrored form.

You were trained backwards.

You don't understand the laws. You don't understand the difference between *reality* and *fiction.* In *man's* world *fiction is form.* In *God's* world *substance is fact.*

God created you *in His image and likeness.* Man created a *form* — an *application-form* for the registration of you body, referred to as an *application for birth certificate* — *the birth report.* But God did not tell you to *register your body to the kings of this world.*

In Scripture, when David took a census of the men, *and numbered them* when he was told not to do so by God, 70,000 Israelites died at the *"hand of the Lord"* because they committed the crime of *registering to the king.* (Ist Chronicles 12:1-14).

The king does not deal with your physical body. He gets you to *register the title of your body to him,* which is a violation of God's law. Now that you have *registered your body to the king,* you have *volunteered your body into slavery* subject to the kings of this world.

When parents *register their child,* through a *security process,* they are *pledging legal title to the child to the state*

— to the kings of this world.

Even though the child may *think he is free,* there is a *security instrument* which represents the *title to the thing in the real world* — the child's body. As far as the lawyers and the kings of this world are concerned, that *security title* (*birth certificate*) is the only thing they see. It's more important to them than *God's reality — the child.*

If they hold the *security — the title —* to little Johnny or little Mary — *if they're the holder-in-due-course of the deed that is the title to the thing* that you thought belonged to you (*your child*) then the state holds legal title to everything *you think you own.* They are playing in *the securities world — the only world that appears to them.*

The term "owner" is not what you think it is. The state told you that you were the *"owner"* of what you own. An *"owner"* has *equitable title* to the thing — not *legal title.*

Legal title gives the holder **total control** of the thing.

Equitable title gives the holder **temporary use and possession** of the thing — temporary possession of *the reality,* but not *possession* of the *security instrument* that represent the *actual legal title to the thing* — the actual property.

Who always wins in court? The *holder of the title,* or the *temporary possessor of the thing?*

The *holder of the title; the actual holder of control.*

Every situation and transaction has two parties — the *creditor* and the *debtor.* Scripture tells us that the *debtor is servant to the master.* The creditor can do no wrong. He has legal title to his *property* (*the thing*) so he can do no wrong.

Your thinking is wrong — you're seeing everything backwards.

If you are not the *creditor,* you are not in control. You gave your control away. You gave your *legal title* away.

A bankruptee does not have *legal title to anything* because *a bankruptee* (by definition) *is a debtor to a creditor.*

The United States *was declared bankrupt — by definition —* in 1933, but the bankruptcy didn't *begin in 1933,* it began in 1782.

In 1782, Benjamin Franklin, Esq., under the authority of the Continental Congress, *signed a six year mortgage with the Crown, in England —* via the first Treaty of Peace after the Revolutionary War — an *acknowledgment* that the Continental Congress had *on twenty-one separate occasions* borrowed a total of 18 million liras from the Crown of England, through the Crown's agent in Paris, the Rothschild Bank.

The Treaty of Peace that *ended the Revolutionary War* was signed in Paris the following year, in 1783.

The *six year mortgage* was to come due on January 1, 1788, and Congress knew they couldn't pay it. So Congress *convened the Constitutional Convention* a year before, to reorganize the government and *give the King of England* a pledge of securities, *to underwrite the debt,* so that the Crown wouldn't *call the Confederate government* due on the loan.

constitution: *a contract in international commerce;* it is not a people thing.

constitutor: *a person who transfers his debts to someone else.* A person is a corporation according to law.

The confederate United States *transferred its debt* to the *states* that became parties to the <u>*Constitutum*</u> of 1787.

Article IV says that all the treaties in existence at the time of the Constitution (1787) are in full force and effect, including the Paris Peace (Debt) Treaty of 1782 when Benjamin Franklin signed the *six year mortgage* of the United States to the Crown. The mortgage was offered to the states and each state accepted it when they ratified the <u>Constitutum</u> for the United States of 1787.

The Crown in England holds a mortgage on all the King's prior colonies (the states) — *a priority agreement* stating that the Crown is the *first creditor* to get paid.

The Founding Fathers *reorganized the bankrupt government* before the debt was due *so they wouldn't have to tell the people what was really being done.* As soon as the Constitution was ratified, George Washington — *under emergency war powers* — went to Congress and created the First National Bank of the United States — a *private* national bank. (Forerunner of the non-federal Federal Reserve).

The purpose of this First National Bank of the United States was to *hold the assets — the securities of the United States — as the pledged collateral on the mortgage.* The bank was a *private third party* that held the assets *to pay off the loan to the Crown of England,* under international law. The bank was the *Receiver for the Crown.*

The creditors were and are now fully in charge.

During the bankruptcy *the creditors run the corporation* called the United States. All the *real officials of the government today are Esquires (as was Benjamin Franklin in his time) — agents for the Crown of England.*

In America today, Crown agents run the legislative, executive, and judicial branches of government as a One World Branch. These Esquires represent the *creditor, the Crown,* during the bankruptcy reorganization of the United States. *They* are complying with the law — *it's us lunatic patriots in America* who are *violating the law* when we criticize our masters who are *legally ruling us under God.*

IN BONDAGE SEVENTY YEARS.

Under International Law, if a nation cannot pay its debts, the debts are forgiven every 70 years.

The number seventy deals with 7 and 10. Seven is *completion,* which is *Sabbatical time for individuals.* You get your debts cancelled in *the seventh year.* But a nation's *Sabbatical time* is *ten times seven or 70 years.*

Seventy years added to 1789, when the mortgage was renewed, comes to 1859. We could have come out of the National Debt in 1859, but the nation *chose to re-enlist in the debt* because of the pending War between the States.

Add 70 years to 1859 and you come to the Great Depression of 1929. We could have come out of the National Debt then, but we didn't because the farmers of America were *forced to pledge their private lands to the public domain* in exchange for public assistance from the banks.

The farmers pledged their land to the National Debt, so the nation continued in debt. Based on the *"presumption* of *regulating and saving farming",* Franklin Delano Roosevelt — *under his emergency war power declarations* — instituted The New Deal and Land Control to overcome the Depression — *and it's still in effect today.*

Add 70 years to 1929, and you come to the *Clinton Impeachment of 1999.*

The Clinton Impeachment didn't deal merely with impeaching Clinton. *It dealt with a Public Notice as to whether or not the People wanted to remain in the bankruptcy to the Crown* — or whether the People wanted to *come out of the bankruptcy and restore the Republic.*

Three periods of 70 years is 210 years in bankruptcy.

The number two-hundred-ten deals with 21 and 10.

Twenty-one is referred to in Scripture as "the time of Jacob's Trouble." *Jacob served 7 years for Laban, 7 years for Lea, and 7 years for Rachel. Ten times 21 years is 210 years* — the time Israel spent in captivity in Egypt.

We are the *New Testament Israel.*

We've been enslaved for 210 years in modern *Egypt* (modern *Babylon*). We were due to come out January 1, 2000, but the people *unknowingly elected* to stay in the bankruptcy to the Crown *and maintain the Democracy.* This is why the United States is going (*big-time*) into the New World Order.

Since the *Public* elected to stay in the bankruptcy after 210 years in captivity, *the People have been given the opportunity to separate themselves from the public domain (and its debt) and become private Freemen* — to come out from under the *bankruptcy of the democracy* through the Redemption-in-Law process. This is what Commercial Redemption is all about.

Only a Remnant will come out. If you are trying to save the United States, it isn't going to happen, it's already lost. But you can *come out of Babylon* before it goes down — *as the Book of Revelation says it will* — and come into the *New Jerusalem; anew.*

"Come out of her, my people, . . . that ye receive not of her plagues." — *Revelation 18:4.*

4
Loyal To The Crown

The government and the judicial system of the United States — at both the federal and local state levels — is owned by the Crown in England.

This is not the Crown of the Queen of England or the Royal Families of Britain. This is a *private foreign power* — *the Templar Church* — known for centuries by the world as the Crown. The Crown is *also* known as the Crown Temple, or the Crown Templar, all three titles being synonymous.

The Temple Church was built by the Knights Templar in two parts, the Round and the Chancel. The Round Church was modeled after the circular Church of the Holy Sepulchre in Jerusalem and was dedicated in 1185. The Chancel was built in 1240. (*note the title, Chancellor*)

The Temple Church serves both the Inner and Middle Temples, and is located between Fleet Street and Victoria Embankment at the Thames River in London. Its grounds house the Crown Offices at Crown Office Row. This Temple Church is *outside* any Canonical jurisdiction. The Master of the Temple is *appointed,* and takes his place by *sealed (non-public) patent,* without induction or institution.

All licensed Bar Attorneys in the U.S. owe their allegiance and swear their solemn oath in pledge to the Crown Temple, whether they realize this or not. All Bar Associations throughout the world are signatories and franchises to the International Bar Association located at the Inns of Court, at Crown Temple, physically located at Chancery Lane behind Fleet Street in London.

Although they strongly deny it, all Bar Associations in the U.S., such as the American Bar Association, the Florida Bar, or California Bar, are franchises of the Crown.

The Inns of Court use the banking and judicial system of the City of London — (a sovereign and independent territory not a part of Great Britain, *just as Washington D.C. is not a part of the North American states, nor is it a state*) — to defraud, coerce, and manipulate the American people.

These Fleet Street bankers and lawyers are committing crimes in America under the guise and color of law. *They are known collectively as "The Crown."* Their lawyers are *actually* Templar Bar "attorneys" not lawyers.

The Queen of England is not the Crown, as we have all been led to believe. Rather, *the Crown is the bankers and "attorneys" who are the actual Crown,* or Crown Temple. The *monarchial aristocrats of England* have not been ruling sovereigns since the reign of King John and the Magna Charta of circa 1215.

All royal sovereignty of the old British Crown — since that time — has passed to the Crown Temple in Chancery.

The U.S.A. is *not the free and sovereign nation that our federal government tells us that it is.* If this were true we would not be dictated to *by the Crown Temple,* through its bankers and attorneys.

The U.S.A. is controlled and manipulated *by this private foreign power,* and our unlawful Federal U.S. Government is their *Pawn Broker.* The bankers and Bar Attorneys in the U.S.A. are a *franchise in oath and allegiance to the Crown and Chancery* — the Crown Temple Church and its Chancel located at Chancery Lane.

The bankers and Bar Attorneys in the U.S.A. are committed in oath and allegiance to a manipulative body of elite bankers and attorneys from the *independent "City of London,"* who violate the law in America by imposing *fraudulent legal — but totally unlawful — contracts* on the American people. The banks rule the Temple Church, and the attorneys carry out their orders by controlling their victim's judiciary.

This is not *a new ruling system* by any means, in that the first Chancel of the Temple Church was built by the Knights Templar. The Chancel, or Chancery, of the Crown Inner Temple Court was the location where King John was based in January 1215 when the English barons demanded that he confirm the rights enshrined in the Magna Charta. This "City of London" Temple was the headquarters of the Templar Knights in Great Britain where Order and Rule were first made which became known as The Code.

"Woe unto you, scribes and Pharisees, hypocrites! for ye are like unto whited sepulchres, which indeed appear beautiful outward, but are within full of dead men's bones, and of all uncleanness." — Matthew 23:27.

By what authority has the Crown usurped the natural sovereignty of the American people?

Is it acceptable to the People that the U.S. Supreme Court decides constitutional issues in the USA? How can it be considered *in any manner "constitutional"* when this same Supreme Court is *appointed* (*not elected*) *and paid for* by the federal government? *The land of North America belongs to the Crown Temple in England.*

The *private non-federal* Federal Reserve System is financially owned and controlled by the Crown, *from Switzer-*

land, the home and legal origin for the Charters of the United Nations, the International Monetary Fund, the World Trade Organization, and — *most importantly* — the Bank of International Settlements.

Even Hitler respected his Crown bankers by *not bombing Switzerland.* The Bank of International Settlements, in Basel, Switzerland, controls all the Central Banks of the G8 nations of the world. He who controls the gold, rules the world.

"Blessed are those that struggle, for oppression is worse than the grave, tis better to die for a noble cause, than to live and die a slave." *— Lost Poets.*

5
Your Name Is Your Bond

Big Brother's Master Plan to subject the human race is entirely dependent upon the people continuing to *volunteer for* and *finance* their own enslavement.

Without such *largess* (*generous giving*) from the public, our chosen masters face the *certain calamity and exposure for their crimes.* Heretofore, system operatives have been overwhelmingly successful at duping unwitting victims into *volunteering* for virtually every kind of financial exploitation imaginable. And it is *all* strictly voluntary.

In 1935 we converted over from *substance backed currency* (*gold*) to *promise backed currency* (*credit*). The objective of *promise backed currency* is to drive all players in the commercial field (*except a favored elite*) into bankruptcy.

Everyone is competing for the same *rationed amount* of Federal Reserve Notes (FRN's) attempting to *stay afloat in a sea of debt* and avoid bankruptcy. This is a *de facto state of commercial war* in the game of life. The only way to stay in the game and avoid bankruptcy is to obtain more FRN's from the other players around you — as in a "Monopoly Game" of life wherein but one party (*the elite*) wins All in the end.

All money is *borrowed into existence* and more money is owed than physically exists because *the principle amount is borrowed but the interest paid on it is not.* Interest payments have to come *from the principle amount borrowed,* thus depleting the money supply *requiring more borrowing* in an never ending spiral into more debt.

The most devastating form of *volunteering* occurs when you promise to be responsible for and pay someone else's debt. This is how the ever unwary individual seals his fate. The "trade-name-game" involves an *unthinking twin* that works hand in hand with it. The legal masters of the world are aware of the distinction between *your true-name* and *your trade-name* and have come up with an ingenious device for exploiting the difference between these two names without tipping their hand.

The reason why the name on every drivers license, social security card, utility bill, etc., *is set in all capital letters — converted from proper English into legalese;* — the reason why all banks insist on listing all accounts *not in the true-name of the party who walks in and fills out the forms* but in *the artificial-trade-name associated therewith* — is to conduct business with you *via your unknown invisible corporately-colored, artificial-person-strawman* that is subject to all their statutory regulations and therefore under their complete control — *regardless of constitutional constraints.* The same applies *equally* when either of the two names *are called out verbally.* Differently constructed names comprise distinctly different items of property *however alike they sound.*

Most people believe that an "appellation" is nothing but an archaic synonym for a "name" — *e.g. "Christian appellation."* The reason people have been generally led to *misunderstand* the meaning of this obscure term is the same reason that Big Brother *calls himself a Sovereign* and *you his subject* under political subjugation — *subject to compelled allegiance to the United States and the British Crown* — when it is actually the other way around. *You are the Sovereign* and Big Brother is *your subject* instead.

Most people believe that when their name is called they are *obligated to respond* — *as though the use of their name exerts control over their lives.* For instance, *calling the role in public school,* taught us to *automatically respond* to any mention of our name.

Your name is a piece of property. It can even be copyrighted so that no one else can use it without your permission and/or paying to you a fee.

You are not your property. You are not your name. An *appellation* is something that originates with someone else. It is a plea for communication. Others use your appellation to address you; to accost you; to get your attention. And how you respond to *such an appeal* is entirely up to you. *Your acknowledgment of your name surrenders jurisdictional power and control to the appealing party.*

People in America have lost sight of the fact that *they are sovereigns* and that nothing can be foisted on them without their *consent* (*agreement*). This is a fact of life. No one can *legally victimize you without your consent.* People have lost sight of *who the boss is* and *who the servant is* and *who they really are.*

Your name is a piece of property. It is not the living, breathing, *flesh-and-blood man* associated therewith. Your name is not you. When someone asks you for your name — *and you give it to him without thinking of the consequences* — you *voluntarily surrender* your *private property* (*your name*) to the other party and *consensually and contractually pre-agree* with whatever he wants to do with it. If he is a judge in court, this can be extremely dangerous.

If you choose to respond *when someone uses your name* (*your common-law-copyrighted-property*) *to get your attention,* you form *an invisible contract with him,* without compensation, *giving him jurisdiction over you* — and *that gift is viewed* as your sovereign, self-determined, *voluntary choice.*

The world operates on the initiative of about 5% of the people (*5 out of each 100*) and the rest of the people need orders to perform.

Such *inert abstractions* as governments, banks, tax agencies, courts, and corporations — *all separate jurisdictional realms* — have been accorded superiority over every living being. Governments are *transitory mental contrivances* set up by the clever few for the purpose of, *for the most part,* living off the efforts of the trusting many.

The entire population of this country, even this planet, *has been systematically deceived through an inconceivably complex mechanism in the field of commerce, law and finance,* by the same tribe of *worldly brilliant sociopaths* who are intent on your subjection and control. But you can begin dealing with the situation from the proper viewpoint *as a self-governing, fully accountable, responsible man or woman* who can control, and is in control, of his or her own destiny — *despite the apparently overwhelming odds stacked against us.*

Knowing that *"you are not your name"* and that you as sovereign *can take legal possession of your name* in all its forms (*like any other piece of private property*) — that the option of accepting or rejecting any appellation from any party that comes your way is strictly yours in your sovereign capacity — *will speed and ease your course in life.*

Your trade-name is your *strawman* and you by default *as its surety* are responsible for knowing and complying with every letter of the law in every situation in existence because *"everyone is presumed to know the law,"* and *"ignorance of the law is no excuse."*

If the *word-manipulators* — who claim the legal title to the strawman with whom you are presumed to be contractually unified — *decide to tax, fine, regulate, rob, incarcerate and maybe even kill you, then you the physical biological being experience the consequences in reality.*

In such capacity as strawman you have no standing in law. A slave cannot sue his master or any other slave because his master owns him.

All of your commercial accounts are in the name of your *strawman-trade-name.* All of your commercial accounts are *your strawman's accounts* not yours. You are the *accommodation party,* the *surety* attached thereto. You are the party that everyone looks to for *payment* and for *performance* because you are the only one capable of paying your strawman's debts — *unless and until you rectify the situation through the Redemption-in-Law process.*

The government accepted *custody of your name* (*your property*) when you were born and registered it via your *original birth record.* Your strawman was *berthed* (*as a vessel*) on the first document emitted by the government referencing your name. Since *everything about you is registered in the name of and accessed by your strawman-trade-name,* all your property is considered to be your strawman's property *as an essential public relations tool for maintaining order within the flock.*

The entire planet functions in a *mirror-image world of unreality* anchored by private money that represents liability — *not substance* — i.e. Federal Reserve Notes (FRN's).

We all live *on the Federal Reserve Plantation* where the Federal Reserve is not an agency of government, *it is a private banking monopoly.* Government has no other way of doing business with you except *via your trade-name-strawman.*

Any presentment to you is *either a demand for payment or for your acceptance — depending upon who you know you are.* In other words, a presentment is *a demand for you to accept responsibility for "paying" (discharging) some charge,* or for the performance of some act.

For instance, a police officer issues a *charge against your strawman (traffic ticket)* demanding you to *accept the responsibility* of the officer's order to your strawman for him to appear and *if necessary* have you pay his ticket — *to discharge the charge.* If at any point in the process the motorist *fails to accept responsibility for his strawman and ultimately pay the ticket (the charge against his strawman)* the motorist is arrested and jailed *in lieu of (in place of)* his strawman.

When anyone in the government demands that you accept responsibility to perform some act *in lieu of your strawman,* he is issuing *a presentment (a bill) and a monetary charge concerning any failure to respond and perform.* Presentments come in written, oral, and electronic form. The acceptance of any presentment *executes a contract* between the *offeror* and the *offeree (the acceptor).*

In the *public sector,* presentments are made by officers of the state. In the *private sector,* presentments are usually made by an attorney, *as an agent of someone else,* since attorneys are officers of the state.

In order for someone to issue a presentment to a strawman, the issuer of the charge must discover *the trade-name of that strawman.* If the issuer cannot discover the *trade-name of a detainee being held for questioning, within a brief period of time,* he must release the detainee and let him go.

The sovereign's trade-name is the *commercial-account-name* under which *the sovereign conducts his business.* The sovereign's *true-name* and his *trade-name* are his private property. *And the sovereign has custody of his private property.*

Any *registration of the trade-name* in the public sector (*via your signature*) constitutes your *voluntary surrender of custody of your private property* to the registrar and the public domain, and *the establishment of a transaction-account in your trade-name.*

When a government official says, *"May I have your name, please?"* he is asking you to *voluntarily surrender your trade-name to him for him to use against you* and to make a charge against *your trade-name-transaction-account.*

Until redeemed, *the flesh-and-blood man (the sovereign) is surety for the party in whose name the transaction-account appears (his strawman)* and is held accountable for any charge leveled against *his strawman's transaction-account.*

Because of the U.S. bankruptcy and the institutionalization *of fiat money (money-by-decree) called Federal Reserve Notes* (FRN's) there have been comparable changes in the realm of jurisprudence.

American tribunals are now *federal-reserve-note-tribunals* dealing exclusively in FRN's and enforcing the *private copyrighted corporate policy of the owners of the FRN's known as public policy and code.* All U.S. Code is *copy-*

righted British law that is owned and copyrighted by British corporations, some on American soil.

The American Revolution of 1776 was never ratified by referendum. Had it been put to a vote by the Founding Fathers, *the so-called rebels would have lost.* Almost all of the Founding Fathers were *Esquires loyal to the British Crown.* The American Revolution was *instigated and financed by the British "front-man-financier" Caron de Beaumarchaise.* (*Nation Geographic Magazine, July 1975, page 114*).

The international bankers *bought* themselves a country: called the United States.

United States: 1) a name, 2) a (British) territory, 3) a collective term. — *Black's Law Dictionary, 6th edition.*

Both criminal and financial charges are commercial in nature. In Admiralty, the Military is used to enforce *criminal penalties for civil offenses.* The money-changers foreclosed on the U.S. government in 1933 and use the U.S. government *to prosecute their private commercial interests.* We are *under military rule* by the Commander-in-chief of the military *re-presented* by the President of the United States.

Under public policy, *which is military rule,* we can be penalized for an act *even when no one is harmed and no property is damaged.* (*e.g. for not wearing a seatbelt, or for travelling 35 mph in a 30 mph zone*).

Under *common law* each man is in control of his own destiny as long as he does not harm another *and thereby form a contract having an obligation.* Under *common law* each man is free to live as he sees fit without interference from government.

Under *public policy* the police power is employed *for penalizing behavior (such as thought crimes)* in addition to acts and deeds of substance — *for the purpose of extorting internal revenue for the state.*

When someone violates his own sense of moral rightness, *no matter how justified in the eyes of the law,* he is weakened under the police power of the state. Therefore it behooves you to *re-assess your life* and begin to use the power of the documents of Redemption-in-Law.

These documents are based on the power of common law, private property rights, and consensual contracts. They are very successful in crushing assaults on your fiscal integrity at both the lower and higher levels of government in this country. They have changed the course of every proceeding in which they have been introduced.

The *common law* still exists and is *in full force,* it is just being covered up and ignored. Never forget that *your name is your private property.*

Therefor learn to guard it well.

6
Registration & Redemption

We are involved in an *official*, undeclared bankruptcy, *nationwide.* This bankruptcy is being prosecuted in open court *publicly for all to see,* yet few have figured it out.

On April 5, 1933 — by an Executive Order of the President — *in order to prevent another Civil War* — Congress passed House Joint Resolution 192 (HJR 192).

In every bankruptcy a *trustee (receiver)* is appointed to represent the *creditor's legal interests* in the bankruptcy. This occurs *tacitly or expressly* without judicial intervention. It's called *reorganization* and occurs *on a minute to minute basis,* wherever and whenever commerce is transacted — wherever and whenever debt is transferred by assignment (*i.e., liability discharged*).

There is no money in circulation. *That which circulates, on confidence alone, is not money,* it is commercial paper.

Redemptors are *creditors* not *debtors.*

Their Treasury Direct Accounts (TDA's) *are prepaid and exempt from levy,* because their human industry — *their labor, their service, their energy* — comes from above; from God; and represents the only wealth that can *discharge this debt ridden society via Redemption in law* — a society *imposed upon us by liars, thieves and warmongers* who are bent on establishing a *Novus Order Seclorum, New World Order.*

Their TDA's are insured, and assume the character of *bonded indebtedness* in order to facilitate the commercial needs of the nation.

Registration

When you were registered with the corporate United States you became a subscribing *member* of the *public corporation* by pledging the *legal interest to all your property as collateral to fund the corporate bankruptcy and keep commerce flowing, and pay the interest on the national debt.*

You *tacitly consented* to what others had done for you in your absence *without your consent.* This is the purpose for *the registration of your birth certificate* and other registrations. This places *the real you* in the capacity of *surety,* or *guarantor,* or *co-signer* for the debts and obligations of *your strawman* — unless, that is, *you've been redeemed* through the Commercial Process of Redemption (CPR).

Redemption

After you have properly *drafted, executed, and "filed for record"* a Commercial Security Agreement (CSA) on a UCC Financing Statement, *you are no longer a debtor to the bankruptcy;* you are a *creditor* of the bankruptcy instead.

As a *creditor,* you can redeem yourself from the consequences of the bankruptcy *by conditionally accepting any presenter's note, draft, charge, or claim* against your strawman. *You hold the highest priority over your strawman.* You are the holder-in-due-course of your strawman and everything that he does.

Fix this fact firmly in your mind: — after Redemption you are a *creditor!* A *creditor* can never lose and a *debtor* can never win. A *creditor* has standing at law and a *debtor* does not.

Bankruptcy

The first rule of bankruptcy is: ***there can be no controversy, no adversarial proceedings, or commercial dishonor ensues.*** Dishonor transforms *the adversary* into *the debtor* who incurs the *liability to pay or perform.* The key to success in bankruptcy is to NOT be advesarial *from the beginning to the end.*

"Blessed are the meek for they shall inherit the earth." (Matthew 5:5).

A Classic Example

The IRS mails you some correspondence using *your strawman's name* (your all uppercase-letter-trade-name).

Their *first objective* is to *bring you into their venue* by your *unconditional acceptance* (receipt) *of their presentment* (their draft). Their *second* objective is to *get you to dishonor their presentment* (their draft) *by contesting it, thereby creating a controversy.* They want you to be *the adversary* (the looser) in the case.

Drafts

A draft is a three-party instrument. It has a *drawer* (the issuer), a *drawee* (the recipient), and a *payee* (the beneficiary).

In the example above, the *agent of the IRS is the drawer of the draft* (the issuer), *your strawman is the drawee* (the recipient), and when redeemed, *you are the payee* (the beneficiary) *of the draft.* As beneficiary, *you receive the value of the draft.* To your strawman *its a charge* (a bill), *but it is an offer of payment to you.* You *dishonor the offer* if you don't accept it as is.

The agent issues the draft *to your strawman* hoping that you will pay it, but *you* think it has been issued to *you*, so *you dishonor it by contesting it* — as incorrect, unconstitutional, or otherwise. This makes you an *adversary subject to the seizure of your goods; not humble and meek.*

Your *dishonor,* or *protest, is* a *counter-offer* which the IRS accepts *and moves against you with* because the IRS is now *the creditor who always wins,* and *you are in default.* This occurs *without any judicial intervention* — in what is called a *non-judicial "lien-foreclosure-sale"* (collection) *under the presiding rules of bankruptcy and the Uniform Commercial Code.*

What to do, what to do . . .

The first thing to do in such a case is to *terminate the presentment* by stating your standing as a *Secured Party Creditor* on the *private side* of the account, because you are the *holder-in-due-course* of your strawman.

This stops the agent from *re-presenting* your interests and imposing *his venue* upon you.

"Accept for value" the draft on the condition that the agent *(the debtor/issuer/drawer)* provide you with *"proof of claim."*

In other words — *"Accept for value"* the presentment on the *condition* that the presenter provides evidence of his legal authority over you or your property *(your strawman).* This he cannot do for he *has no* such authority. As *Redemptor,* you hold the highest priority over your *strawman.* You're its *holder-in-due-course.*

In bankruptcy, the *creditor* has the right to require **"proof of [the] claim"** or *charge,* but this right must be exercised properly or you will *traverse (argue)* into the public jurisdiction and venue where prosecution of the bankruptcy can only occur.

Do your *"acceptance"* in a Notice of Claim; exercise your Right under the authority of **31 USC 5118** to *discharge* the liability — *all principal, penalties and interest* — to balance the account to zero. Demand that the *order* for the adjustment of the account be released to you, the *creditor,* for discharge.

You have then *discharged the debt* and are no longer under the jurisdiction and authority of strangers.

Your *conditional acceptance* constitutes *a counter-offer* to *their offer,* namely *a redraft of their draft,* which represents a retail installment contract whereby *you give* them *your credit* so they cannot qualify you for the debt — and *presto,* the charge is discharged (*zeroed out*) (*balanced*).

It's as simple as that.

— — —

But simply pledging birth certificates is insufficient to turn free men into debtor/slaves without their consent. This is accomplished more subtly, for several reasons. The most significant reason for hiding what is going on is that *"the most productive slaves are slaves who <u>believe</u> they are free."*

So you continue the *propaganda about freedom* in the now bankrupt nation because it makes debt collection much easier by far.

In all likelihood, your name is spelled properly on your birth certificate. If you immigrate to The United States, the Visa will also be issued in your real name. This seems quite odd, especially as it gets placed within the pages of a Passport that has only the ALL CAPS name in it.

Immigration, it turns out, is really transferring yourself as an asset from one nation to another, and it will be the State of the UNITED STATES, not the nation of the United States of America that considers you of sufficient value to be accepted as one of theirs, for bankruptcy collection and settlement purposes. Once here, you will be promptly turned over to the State of the UNITED STATES for management, and all other documents will be issued only to your artificial PERSON/STRAWMAN.

So if you look on the title to your house or vehicle, you will see that it has the ALL CAPS name on it, meaning it is not really owned by you at all, but by the creditors of the bankrupt, corporate UNITED STATES. The artificial PERSON/STRAWMAN is a fiction, and a fictitious entity CANNOT own anything.

7

Adminitrative Law

The UCC is Administrative Law that provides the rules for all commercial transactions. When one files under the UCC there is no controversy, hence no court can become involved. The artificially contrived *system* is impotent when faced with an unlimited liability sovereign (*a chief ruler with supreme power*).

One accesses Commercial law by the simple process of asserting one's solemn oath *"sworn true, correct, and complete"* on one's <u>un</u>limited, commercial liability as a real flesh-and-blood, sentient being.

The first and critical step is to redeem the legal title (*ownership*) to your corporately colored *property* identified as the all-capital-lettered *trade name* that was *birthed* and registered as you on your birthday — your strawman.

Legal Freedom

What you *do* know can't hurt you because you can use your knowledge of the truth to *"set yourself free"* (*John 8:32*). But what you *do not* know can get you killed. Ignorance is potential suicide. Do not consent to being enslaved if you do not wish to be enslaved.

Contract

All law is contract. Contract makes the law. To make a contract valid, the *consent* of the parties must be *free, mutual,* and *communicated.* Consent is not *real* or *free* when obtained through *duress, menace, fraud, undue influence* or *mistake.*

The crucial and incurable flaw in all contracts is the absence of *full disclosure* and a *true meeting of the minds* — and *mutual good faith*. This constitutes *fraud*. Lenders do not disclose the fact that they do not loan out their funds. They do not operate in *good faith*. They are collection agents on contracts that are deceitfully devised and incomplete. There is usually no *genuine agreement* between the parties based on truth.

The Deceit

In order for a contract to be valid it must be entered into with *full disclosure, good faith,* and *clean hands.*

However, the banks (*and other lending institutions*) lead you to think that you borrow *their* money and give them the right to your property should you default. What they willfully, intentionally and deceitfully do not disclose is the fact that member banks of the Federal Reserve are not allowed to make loans. They simply exchange your promise for another promise; no legal tender (*cash*) changes hands.

You promise to pay a sum of money to the bank over a period of time, *plus interest* — you sign a promissory note — and the bank promises to credit your account with debt obligations — *fiat money.* You create the 'money' when you sign the promissory note — *the loan agreement; the credit card agreement, etc.* — and give it to the bank, then *they* in turn give the money *you* created by your signature (*in signing your note*) back to you, with *interest* and *property claims* attached. We call this *"The Bait & Switch."*

Your promissory note is posted on the banks books as a *debt* that you will have to repay. But this *debt* and its *usury obligation* and its *claims* against your property (*collateral*) is obtained by the bank under false pretenses with no *con-*

sideration (*real money*) involved. The bank converts your *signature* (*your asset*) into a *liability* (*a debt*) that you will have to pay to them over time, *plus interest.* If you fail to do so, the bank will take your property (*your collateral*) from you.

You allow the bank to take *your property* (*your signature*) and *give it back to you* in a changed form, *with strings attached.* Your promissory note is evidence of the bank's claim against your future labor. Moreover, the bank usually sells your promissory note *up-front* for cash. Then when they collect your payments they get paid *again.* And if you *default,* they will foreclose on your property and get paid a *third* time when they sell it at discount to someone else.

You take all the risk. For the bank to put your property at risk without *full disclosure, good faith,* or *clean hands* is the equivalent of *plunder, counterfeiting,* and *theft.* The bank does *not* loan you *their* money; they *sell your note* and give *your money* to you, expecting you to give it back to them in payments . . . *plus interest.*

The bank does *not* loan you money; it loans you **your credit** instead.

Remedy: Offer & Acceptance

offer: *n* 1. The act or instance of presenting something for acceptance. 2. A display of willingness to enter into a contract on specified terms, made in a way that would lead a reasonable person to understand that an acceptance having been sought will result in a binding contract.

acceptance: *n* 1. An agreement, either by express act or implication from conduct, to the terms of an offer so that a binding contract is formed.

If an acceptance modifies the terms or adds new terms, it operates as a counter-offer, not an acceptance.

When you send a check marked "final payment" on an account you are making an offer for the bank to accept. The bank can respond in two ways.

1. If the bank *cashes* your negotiable instrument marked "final payment" it is accepting your offer (*claim*) that it is a final payment ; it is agreeing with you on your terms.

2. If the bank *refuses* to accept your negotiable instrument marked "final payment" then your account is legally *paid in full* anyway in accord with the UCC.

UCC 3-603 says that when a tender of payment to a person entitled to enforce the instrument is made, the effect of the tender is governed by the principles of law that apply to a simple contract. If the tendered payment is refused, there is discharge of liability for the payment debt. The debt is now transferred to the one who refuses to accept the instrument.

maxim: A payment tendered and refused is paid in full.

Under HJR-192 (*House Joint Resolution 192*) passed by Congress in 1933, and still in force today, it is public policy not to *pay* a debt. It is impossible to do so now with real money. No person can compel anyone to *pay* the debt by tendering silver or gold. Once a debt is *created* it is never extinguished. Its *obligation* (*liability*) is simply *discharged* — the debt is transferred from one party to the next.

With the advent of the bankruptcy and HJR-192 in 1933, it became no longer necessary — or required — to *pay* a debt. It is only necessary to *discharge the liability set forth,* when it becomes due, by tendering *another* negotiable instrument by which the sum tendered (*being sufficient in amount*) discharges the liability in the underlying instrument.

Offer and Acceptance

maxim: The *offeror* is the *tail* & the *acceptor* is the *head.*

maxim: You must go *low* to be made *high.*

"For whosoever exalteth himself shall be abased; and he that humbleth himself shall be exalted." — *Jesus at Luke 14:10,11.*

maxim: When an *offer* is refuse it is *dishonored.*

An Offer — being a presentment of something for acceptance — commands a response. And, there are *three ways* in which a person can respond. He can [1] *accept* the offer as stated, [2] present a *counter-offer,* or [3] *stand mute.* If he stands mute his silence is *acceptance* of the claim. A *counter-offer* must be a claim of a *higher priority* than the offer presented.

Novation

novation: n 1. The act of substituting for an *old* obligation a *new* obligation that either replaces an *existing* obligation with a *new* obligation or replaces an *original* party with a *new* party. (*it is a substitute agreement*). 2. The substitution of a *new obligor* for a *previous obligor* who has been discharged by the *obligee.*

It's called a *novation* when you place yourself (*as a new obligor*) in the position of your strawman (*the previous ob-*

ligor) who has been discharged by the *Redemption-in-Law process*. Your strawman is replaced by you in the agreement and no claim can be made against you or your strawman because you have both been redeemed. Such a claim would *"fail to be a claim upon which relief can be granted."*

"Agree with thine adversary quickly, while thou art in the way with him; lest at any time the adversary deliver thee unto the judge, and the judge deliver thee unto officer, and thou be cast into prison.

Verily I say unto thee, Thou shalt by no means come out thence, till thou hast paid the uttermost farthing."
— *Jesus at Matthew 5:25,26.*

8
Ye Shall Be As Gods

The Elevation of Man into the ranks of the gods of the world is now taking place. Those who are planning to remake our world after their own images — when they are ready to — will create economic conditions that will cause the world's economies to collapse.

The original Marxist plan was to establish a privately owned Central Bank in each nation of the world. These banks would issue the currency and set its interest rates for their own profit and gain.

Just as Albert Pike's 1871 plan — *of many revolutionary wars and three world wars* — is about complete, so is Lenin's plan — *of first taking Eastern Europe, secondly the masses of Asia, and thirdly "surrounding the United States and it would fall"* — nearly complete. Each plan is on schedule today.

When they are ready to come into their kingdom, the elite will gather to themselves monopolies. They will then "pull the plug" on the artificially high stock markets of the world. This will create panic and lead to a worldwide economic collapse.

At this point, military troops will be needed to work in conjunction with the police to prevent or contain riots and the breakdown of society. With an economic collapse, little food processing and distribution can take place; even the planting and harvesting of crops will be most difficult. That's why the Third Horse of Revelation 6 tells us not to misuse food, and to use our money wisely, when this man-made collapse takes place.

It will be the International Bankers who have wormed their way into the control of the money systems of each country, who will cause the collapse — several super-rich families who produce nothing; but spend US4 cents to print any denomination of money, and receive full value for it.

The Federal Reserve Act, that was passed by Congress in 1913, in America, *gave* these banker-families — J. P. Morgan, the Rothschilds, the Rockefellers, etc. — the exclusive "right" to print f$1, f$2, f$5, f$10, f$20, f$50, f$100, (etc.), bills for 4 cents each. They in turn loan this fiat money to our government, and charge interest on the loans.

What's more, the Federal Reserve's Central Bank never prints enough money to pay the interest! Therefore, you can *never* pay off the principle *and* the interest, if only the principle is ever printed. The interest has to be taken from the labored wealth of the people. When we hear politicians talk of paying down the national debt, they are talking "foolery" and lies.

The Federal Reserve is neither federal nor a reserve bank. President Ronald Reagan, in his first address to the nation in 1981, said that the Federal Reserve is an autonomous profit making organization that sets interest rates for their own purposes.

Allen Greenspan, head of the Federal Reserve, increased interest rates 6 times in the year 2000 to stop Americans from prospering. A recession, or severe slowdown in the economy, was the intended result. Now that the Feds have sent the stocks down so their agents could buy up the good stocks at reduced prices, Greenspan has lowered interest rates 3 times in 2001, through March.

These world government plotters have created stock

exchanges around the world, and created "interdependence" of nations at the same time. Why have they done this? Because they cannot create a worldwide economic collapse that will effect every person upon the earth unless all nations and stock markets are interdependent.

In 1897, this group of Conspirators said they would cause the markets to crash *after* they had accumulated all the gold — wealth — into their hands. This they did for the first time in the late 1930s, and they intend to do it once again. On the heels of this *second* collapse, they expect the people to cry out for a "savior." They intend to have their man waiting in the wings to step onto the world stage, claiming, in so many words, to be God. They used the term *apotheosis,* which means elevation of a man into the ranks of the gods. This is verified in 2 Thes. 2:4 and Daniel 11:31-36 in the Holy Bible.

The world has been divided up into 10 global groupings of nations along economic and political lines, on a computer model, by a world government think tank — the Club of Rome. It is interesting to note that Daniel 2:36-45 indicates "economics" to be a vital part of the last social system before Christ comes to establish His Kingdom. Revelation 13:11-18 also clearly demonstrates that economics will divide the world into believers in Christ — Christians — and believers in the Antichrist economic system that has now taken place.

Do you believe Communism is dead? Do you believe there is no push for world government based upon the Marxist theories of redistribution of the people's wealth? Do you believe that the *United Nations* is a sincere effort by "good" men and women to create a more just and equitable world? Do you believe *Socialism* in America is dead? Your wrong.

Socialism is a step that every nation must achieve before pure Communism can be installed upon every nation. The Bill Clinton impeachment and its abortment will have deadly serious consequences for America. Nothing this serious has happened politically since the American War between the States in 1861-1865.

The class struggle between the super-rich and we-the-people is still going on. War in secret is still being waged. They created the problem — possible total extinction — and are furnishing their solution — merging Capitalism and Communism into a One World Government with only ONE military so no one can ever disturb the peace again.

A chained people cannot revolt.

9

The Obligation Of Contracts

"No State shall ... pass any ... law impairing the obligation of contracts." — *U.S Constitution, Article 1, Section 10.*

OUR MANAGERS have enslaved us by an end run around our constitutional rights. They devised a scheme that enables them to dominate us as their slaves. And this is how their deceitful scheme works.

Based on the constitutional stipulation that *"No State shall ... pass any ... law impairing the obligation of contracts"* (*epigram above*) — and in order to provide goods and services for the people and end the Great Depression of 1929-1933 — the bankrupt government of the United States created a commercial bond (*contract; promissory note*) for each citizen of America by pledging his or her energy, labor, property, life and limb as collateral for the nation's ever increasing never ending debt. This commercial bond made chattel (*commercial property; slaves*) out of every man, woman, and child in America — without our knowledge or consent.

How? Through filing (*registering*) our birth certificates with the Department of Commerce as registered securities (*warehouse receipts*), each of which carries an estimated value of US$1 million (FRN's) to be circulated around the world as *collateral* for loans — *simple entries* on the asset and debit sides of ledgers, just like any other security, except without our knowledge or consent.

The United States is now a debtor corporation — a foreign corporation with respect to any state. Since a corporation is a *fictitious "person,"* it cannot by itself function in the real world — it therefore needs *a liaison* of some sort — *a transmitting utility* — to connect it (*as fictional entity*) to the real world.

Living people exist in the *real world* — not in the *fictional world* of the government where the government can only deal with other *fictional persons, agencies, states, etc.* In order for a *fictional person* (*corporation*) to deal with *real people* there must be a *liaison* — *a connection.* This can be accomplished with something as simple as a contract.

When both persons, the real and the fictional, agree to the terms of a contract there is *a connection* — communication — an exchange — there is *intercourse* — there is *commerce* — there is *business.*

Another way for fictional government to deal with the real man and woman — *constitutionally but outside of constitutional restraints* — is through a *representative* — a *go-between agent.* Who is this go-between agent? It's a government created *fictional man or woman* with the same name as yours. This fictional person is a *strawman* created by the state by regarding your birth certificate as your *Manufacturers Certificate of Origin* (MCO) and the state in which you were born as your *Port of Entry* (POE) into the commercial venue.

This *strawman* is a front — a third party who is put forward in name only to take part in and transact your business in your stead, *without your interference, knowledge or control* — one who acts as a government agent in your behalf (*actually in the government's behalf*) for the purpose of taking title to real property — an imaginary *supposedly passive* stand-in — a front — a blind — *a shadow go-be-tween.*

Since all so-called money is *evidence of debt* — evidence of the *public (national) debt* — there is no *positive* side to the ledger, only the *negative* side; only the debt. But there are still two sides to the ledger.

There are only *two classes* of citizen in the United States — *debtors* on the public side and *creditors* on the private side. On the public side is the *public debt* that the debtors are obligated to repay but never able to repay. On the private side is the *private debt* that the creditors are promised to receive and someday will receive. The only transaction between the two sides of the ledger (*to keep score*) are the *charges* and *discharges* of the *digits-of-debt* from one side to the other in a never-ending shuttling back and forth of commercial intercourse.

The national debt that the government has borrowed in our strawmen's names (*supposedly for our benefit*) is posted on the *public side* of the ledger as *public debt* owed by the debtors to the creditors, and on the *private side* as *private debt* owed to the creditors.

Your strawman's portion of the *public debt* is posted as an entry on the public side of the ledger, a liability owed by you (*as your strawman's co-signer*) to your strawman's creditor — the United States Congress — who in turn owe it to the non-federal Federal Reserve, and a few others whoever they may be. Your strawman is owned by the government of the United States, by way of an *assumed contract* based on the government's *presumption of ownership* of your strawman. Since *silence is acceptance of the presumption,* you are obligated — as a co-signer for your strawman — for everything he does and everything he owes to his creditor, the corporate government of the United States. This makes you *a serf* — *a slave* — *an employee* of the government of the corporate United States.

The plans for our centralized banking system, the non-federal Federal Reserve, were laid in 1910 and came into existence three years later when Congress passed the Federal Reserve Act in 1913.

Between 1910 and 1913 the national debt of the United States *grew* from $2.6 billion to $2.9 billion, an increase of but 10%. But between the time that the Federal Reserve was established in 1913, and the *climax* of the Great Depression in 1929, the Federal Government *expanded* the national debt from $2.9 billion to $17 billion! an increase of more than 500%!

During that brief 15 year period, the U.S. Government payed the interest on its debt to the Federal Reserve in gold — (*there is no requirement for the principle ever to be paid back*) — until the United States had no more gold left. So when the Federal Reserve offered to extend the U.S. Government all the credit it would *ever* need — *if it would reorganize itself under Chapter 11 Bankruptcy by contractual agreement* — this is what the government did. The government could *then* borrow an unlimited amount of credit digits, so this is what it did and continues to do today.

Four years later, on April 5, 1933, President Franklin Delano Roosevelt declared a *"national emergency";* took the nation off the gold standard; and seized all the county's remaining gold, for the Federal Reserve — and replaced *legitimate, constitutional rule* with *the obligation of contracts, "Public Policy."*

Since 1933, the U.S. Government has mixed together, *public, private,* and *martial law* practices and rules.

Roosevelt's executive order (EO) was *not deemed* by Congress to be the act of Treason that it was, because — *since executive orders were directives or instructions to officers or employees of the federal government, only* — Congress classified the *general public* to be government *employees.*

On June 5th — two months after the fact — the 73rd Congress passed House Joint Resolution 192 (HJR-192) *"to suspend the gold standard and abrogate the gold clause to assure uniform value to the coins and currency of the United States."*

HJR-192 *superceded Public Law* and replaced it with *Public Policy.* This removed our ability to pay our debts (*Revelation 13:17*) requiring only their *discharge* — passing the unpaid debt on to another person by our trade. Under Public Policy, *this unpaid debt* carries *a never ending public liability for its discharge.* In other words, all interest on the national debt is now payed on the basis of *a perpetual ever increasing unpayable public debt.*

Because it was *bankrupt* and there was no longer any legal money after 1933 (*i.e., gold and silver*), the US *government needed some other way to pay its* interest (*insurance*) *payments* to the Federal Reserve. It did this by seizing the *energy* of the country, including the *energy* produced by its *citizen/employees.*

With the advent of Social Security in 1936, the US government began to register birth certificates with the Department of Commerce *as marketable securities* representing the *energy, labor and skills* of each citizen, and everything each citizen owned or would ever own.

A *pledge* was made for each certificate in the amount of $630,000 as a bond to be sold on the open market to finance the government and its debt. Everybody in the United States is *collateral chattel* — now valued at $1,000,000 — to insure that the *interest* on the bonds issued by the US government are paid.

When you were born, the state became the recipient of your *future energy output* as a *title-security document*, which the state converted into a bond sold on the *open market* to finance the government. The *holder* of that bond is the *secured party* to your future energy output.

Does the bondholder own you? Not quite. He owns *the fruits of you labor.* He owns the *results* of everything you do. Each person (*in fact*) has a mirror entity which represents this *energy output.* It is called your *"nom de guerre"* — your *strawman.* JOHN DOE is different from John Doe. JOHN DOE is not you; it's your *mirror entity strawman* — set up to represent *your energy output.*

Every man, woman and child has a strawman. When you sign *your name* to something, you are co-signing for your *strawman* and putting property into the hands of the United States and its bond owners, not into your own hands.

There are two types of citizen in America: *14th Amendment citizens* subject to the policies, laws and taxes of the federal and state governments; and *sovereign denizens* — subject only to public common law.

The Redemption-in-Law process gives *Redemptors* a way to use this situation to their advantage. It provides a means for taking control of your strawman. Once you control your strawman, then you control the rights and titles to the property that your strawman acquires in your behalf, and a whole lot more. You are then *free* from *the land of the "fee" and home of the "slave".*

10
Why The Redemption Process Works

THE UCC FINANCING STATEMENT is the only *unbreakable contract* in the world. It is the ultimate foundation, the bedrock, upon which the world's commerce functions.

No lawful money
There is no lawful money in circulation today. What passes as *money* — the medium of exchange, currency, legal tender — is *private, commercial paper* evidencing the debt of the citizens of the country to pay on the collective bankruptcy of the government.

Real money is *substance* (*gold, silver, tangible produce of the earth, including labor*), it cannot be debt. "Citizen" = bankrupt = legal incapacity = no rights of title to anything = no ownership of self or property = no right to own, use, or pass *real money*.

The use of real money is the right of *sovereigns,* not slaves. This is why House Joint Resolution 192 (HJR-192) of June 5, 1933, in declaring the bankruptcy of the United States corporation, states: *"...every provision contained in or made with respect to any obligation which purports to give the obligee a right to require payment in gold or a particular kind of coin, or currency, or in an amount in money of the United States measured thereby, is declared to be against Public Policy."*

In line with the bankruptcy of the US Government, HJR-192 outlawed the payment of debts in gold or silver, and provides only for the *"discharge"* of debts in *"legal tender"* meaning Federal Reserve Notes (FRNs). Federal Reserve Notes are *permanently unfulfilled, irredeemable, evidences of debt,* private commercial scrip — fiat money (*money by government decree*).

Public Policy

Public Policy = "Federal Reserve *re-insurance policy.*" Every time a budget is passed by a government legislature, or assets are *pledged or hypothecated* (*which happens billions of times a day in the world*), existing insurance policies are *re-insured.* Commerce, existing in admiralty, is in a state of *perpetual flux,* it is *ever-changing,* like waves of the sea.

This renders every "Citizen of the United States" *civilly dead* in the law. It bars the way back to the *Eden of Sovereignty;* of power to enforce one's rights; of access to true common law, etc. It leaves everyone *bound* to the *ever-shifting mirage of endless hypothecations against your strawman* over which no other one should have a claim but you.

Money (d*ebt*) is created by *one's signature;* by signing *notes of indebtedness.* All *money* in circulation today is *created* out of thin-air by borrowing against the collective, federal bankruptcy. Only by borrowing against a *government's bankruptcy* can its citizen-slaves have pieces of paper (*monopoly money*) to spend like money.

Unless you are the *"holder-in-due-course"* (HDC) of your strawman, *owning* such debt money or anything it buys is *a liability;* not an asset. The fact that people *mistakenly* consider FRNs (*Federal Reserve Notes*) to be assets — that the more of them one acquires the *richer* one is, — is a major cause of the problem. When you accumulate FRNs, you are accumulating *debt*. The more FRNs — the more industrial goods and services you acquire with them — the more you are in debt to the *non-federal Federal Reserve*.

Since *all money* is created by borrowing against a nation's *collective bankruptcy, by signature*, every time you sign your name to any public document, contract, or instrument involving FRNs as the *"valuable consideration,"* you *borrow against* (*increase*) your own debt to the Federal Reserve. By increasing your borrowing and indebtedness you provide yourself with more *debt instruments* to "spend." This is akin to a slave in *permanent indentured servitude* who commits himself to *ever-deepening debt* every time he borrows from his master in order to have scrip to use to purchase goods and services at the plantation store.

Since *all money is created by borrowing against the collective bankruptcy of the corporate United States,* it is mathematically impossible to ever *pay off* the ever accumulating National Debt. The only money available must be borrowed into existence. Thus any *money* one acquires to *pay* on the *interest of the debt* has to be obtained by borrowing and *increasing* the very debt one is attempting to pay off. This is a *never-ending, ever worsening,* situation. To see this principle in action, examine the rate of increase of the National Debt. The people's debt made them *slaves to the plantation store* in the first place. The *cure* is not *more* of the disease.

When you establish your sovereignty and self-ownership in law, via filing a *UCC Financing Statement,* your entire life is dramatically affected for the good. You become the HDC, or *the sovereign,* rather than a *hopeless debtor* and *chattel property* of the Federal Reserve. The controversy, fighting, arguing, dodging, *paying,* and fear are over.

Summary

The State (*in any aspect, any jurisdiction, any country, any culture, at any time*) can act against your strawman *only* if the said State holds *title* to it by virtue of your *failure to redeem it.* Your *failure* constitutes *assent* to the presumption that the State is the *"de facto"* (*in fact only*) owner and holder of the *title* to your strawman.

The most powerful contract in the world is a *UCC Financing Statement.* It is impenetrable — and the *foundation of all commerce.*

The *hidden* Financing Statement currently in place against your life, your labor, and all your property was established by the State by *illegitimate presumption.* You are in the adverse condition that you're in today because you have failed to *rebut the presumption.*

The *security instrument,* to which the bankers presently hold title, is your *birth certificate.* Your are their *collateral.* This happened only as a result of your failure to rebut their presumption to the contrary.

The bankers have conquered and enslaved the world *only* because of the ignorance, apathy, and default of each slave. This is a *free-will universe.* The *"unit"* of experience, choice, rights, and sovereignty is each *individual free-will man or woman.* You are the *only being* in the world with either the right, knowledge, or duty to speak for yourself — no one else can assert your rights for you. If you *fail to assert your rights,* you have *tacitly agreed* to be a slave, subject to the whims of your masters.

You must understand that the bankers' claim of ownership of *title to your strawman,* via your birth certificate, *is by presumption only,* and only stands because of your *failure* to rebut it. Filing a *UCC Financing Statement* against your strawman rebuts *any presumptive claim* to your strawman by anyone other than yourself ; while at the same time being itself *un-rebuttable.*

There are many reason for this, the most *crucial reason* being that any substantiation of a *"bona fide"* (*authentic*) *contract* between you as king and the usurpers of your throne is impossible, because *there never was a "bona fide" contract* due to the absence of *true agreement,* because the supposed interaction is *devoid of full disclosure, a genuine meeting of the minds,* and *mutual good faith.*

You are — and are *correctly presumed* to be in law — a foundational, original unit of sovereignty. Whatever you choose to do, or not do, is presumed to be done, or not done, *by your free choice.* If you fail to rebut their presumption that you are subject to their system, they *presume* that you chose to act as you do with knowledge of the law in the free-will manner that you did. *"Ignorance of the law is no excuse."*

Conversely, the same system that has worked *against* you, can now work *for you* when you *rebut their presumption* and redeem the sovereign capacity that you have lost. Approximately six billion people are *"ex-sovereigns"* who have — *by their sovereign act of in-action* (*default*) — made themselves *slaves on the slave plantation* of which they are the *actual, rightful* owners.

The 1939 movie, *The Wizard of Oz,* is an allegory of how the American people had just been scammed out of their sovereignty and gold, showing how easy it is *to con the people* with a little slight of hand; illusion; a "light-show." Just as the Wizard fooled Dorothy and her friends in the beginning of the movie with his light-show, nearly all of the six billion people referred to herein have been *artfully conned* out of their sovereignty by the *real Wizard* : *the Apocalypse Beast.* Most of the world has enslaved itself by belief in an *Apocalypse Mirage* — an illusion.

You can rebut the system's *presumptive claim* against you by filing — in your real, biological, sovereign capacity — a UCC Financing Statement and Private Security Agreement in the office of any state's Secretary of State, claiming title to your strawman. You can also secure all other items you wish to maintain dominion over and own, under your UCC Financing Statement by filing a UCC Financing Statement Amendment. Then *the system* can *perfect no claim* against you or your strawman or any of the secured property you list.

A *subject* or *slave* has no capacity to assert any rights at all, and *the system* has the legally, contracted right to treat you any way it wills. On the other hand, a *sovereign* holds *sovereign title* to his property. When you *re-claim self-ownership* of yourself, neither the bankers, nor anyone else in existence, can perfect any claim against you in a court of law.

In law, one is either a *complete slave* (*debtor*) or *unalloyed sovereign* (*creditor*); there is no middle ground. All actions, other than eliminating *the system's* false presumption of ownership of you, leaves you subject to the un-rebutted presumption of that claim. Anything (*such as the huge maze and light-show of governments, courts, and quasi-common law*) other than the elimination of *the system's* illegitimate *presumptuous ownership* of you, leaves you in the same condition of being a debtor-slave.

You may ask: *"Since they are criminals, what is to prevent them from disregarding these legal processes and acting against me anyway?"*

Well, the *powers-that-be* achieved their current status as rulers of the world, after having meticulously scrutinized the law over many *millennia*. This was done to make and *keep the system* legal.

Like a coin, every aspect of existence has two sides. This applies to all laws, rules, and regulations. If any laws are utilized in *one way,* they can also be used in the *opposite way.* If any laws are used *against* you by default, they can also be used *to your advantage* when used correctly. *The law always provides a remedy.* They must leave you *a way out,* or blow all cover of legitimacy and legal authority. In such an event, they announce that *they are merely thugs,* and thereby give you the full right in the law from time immemorial *to self-defense.* In such a case, *all law (including "thou shalt not kill") would be over-ruled by the "law of necessity" — survival.*

No tyrant can rule without the broad-based assent of the people. Power always has and always will reside in *we-the-people.* People become slaves because they choose *to give their power away,* rather than retain it. No tyrant can attain a position of rulership and keep it if a sufficient number of people *become aware of the truth* and re-claim or assert their inherent power.

The laws of commerce are now *inviolate* and *established* throughout the world. Even *martial law* exists within the confines of commercial law.

Once you have filed a *UCC Financing Statement,* establishing the *real, sovereign you* as the *Secured Party,* you have the exclusive and only claim on your strawman. You are then, *"first-in-line and first-in-time."* You work in *tandem* with your strawman and no one can get to either of you. This renders you *legally sovereign, free,* and immune from all public claims and charges.

This scenario prevails because the world has been set up to run *precisely in this way,* only we (*slaves*) were not supposed to figure it out.

Before the bankruptcy, sovereigns were personally accountable for their actions in courts which were set up to accommodate disputes among sovereigns, such as the original common law courts in England before 1066. *Now,* the people's strawmen, which are *the legally owned property of the system,* are subject parties as adjudicated and enforced by *the system.* Such *former sovereigns* are now *personally accountable* for their strawmen because they are inextricably joined with them, although their strawmen are owned *via implied contract* by a handful of arch-charlatans; the elite.

Courts today are set up to deal *only* with strawmen. We — their unfortunate counterparts — are merely *"along for the ride."* A *sovereign* (*real being*) has no place in a commercial court dealing in artificial persons — and *cannot* be legally accommodated.

Only if the current *debt-based system of finance and government* is rectified, will we ever get back to a sane and just basis for the resolution of disputes, and a sound civilization.

Make your *spiritual life* preeminent. *"Seek ye first the Kingdom of God and His righteousness and all these things shall be added unto you."* Or, as a great Indian sage, stating the matter, said: *"Seek the highest first."* This means, *"inter alia"* (*among other things*), maintain your integrity and ethical behavior. In practice, this requires that you keep your word, honor your contracts, and not depart from your principles.

A fundamental flaw in man's thinking is the notion that he can cheat moral or natural law (*usually by trying to cheat others*) and get away with it. Every such attempt generates inexorable cause and effect consequences — all man's philosophies, systems, and cleverness to the contrary, notwithstanding.

Our *predicament* is due to our failure to live in harmony with and according to natural and moral law. The current system is the result of our own folly. All governments are expressions of and exist by virtue of the people's *irresponsibility, ignorance, laziness, larceny,* and their *surrender of personal power, freedom, and autonomy* in exchange for *"being taken care of."*

In other words, every government exists due to the *express will,* as well as *implied default,* of the people — combined with the willingness of ruthless tyrants to accept and manage the surrender of the people's power to a fictitious, artificially created, so-called "government."

As Joseph de Maistre noted: *"Every country gets the government it deserves."*

HARDCORE REDEMPTION-IN-LAW

11

The Commercial System

Definitions

commerce:— Each and every *interchange* between people is commerce. Commerce includes but is not limited to sexual intercourse, the exchange of thoughts and ideas, and the ordinary buying and selling of goods in the market place, to which the term commerce is commonly applied.

law is contract: — Every interchange between people is by contract; all commerce is by contract. It is a timeless and universal maxim of law that *"contract makes law."*

chattel: — *All moveable personal property;* including a slave.

commercial chattel: — Property. A slave or *permanently indentured servant* is commercial property: chattel; by contract and the operation of commercial law.

law: — *The body of rules* that define who possesses the authority to use deadly force against another.

The legal status of every man, woman, and child on this planet is basically that of a slave, a piece of commercial chattel-property; a hopelessly indentured servant, forever. In law it is an all-or-nothing situation; you are either a slave or a sovereign (*a sovereign is a monarch; a king, queen, or other supreme ruler*). There is no middle ground; you are either one or the other; you are either a slave or a sovereign. If you want the power in law to exercise your God given sovereignty, you must *actualize* the laws which enable you to be recognized *in law* as a sovereign.

Redemption-in-Law is a set of procedures that enables you to have your God given freedom and sovereignty recognized in and by law.

Preamble

For thousands of years the *powers-that-be* have been steadfastly constructing *the system* by which world law and commerce now operate. They developed *the system* utilizing timeless principles of human interaction which over the millennia have been discovered and then codified. These common-sense principles underlie every form of law on this planet. Every legal issue and dispute deals with one or more of these fundamental principles. Since all *human interchange* is commerce, in order for the elite to rule people, it is now only necessary for them to govern the commerce by which the people interact and subsist; to *allow them to,* or *prevent them from* "buying" and "selling" in the market place. Those operating *the system* have achieved their preeminence by knowing the *foundational principles* and then *obfuscating them* by encrypting them into *"codes"* for their benefit, while confusing the masses and keeping them *ignorant* of such real law and how to apply it correctly. The *pinnacle* of their efforts is the *Uniform Commercial Code.*

World commerce now functions under and is securely entrenched in the UCC. The important points to remember are that while the UCC was formulated for purposes of *exploitation and subjugation,* it is a codification of the universal underlying principles and laws of commerce, and more importantly, it can be *employed* for our benefit, now that *"the Code"* has been *"cracked."*

Commercial Law Maxims

The foundational *maxims* of the commercial code from which all law and commerce in the world today is derived, are as follows:

1. **A workman is worthy of his hire.**
2. **All are equal under the law (*moral & natural law*).**
3. **In commerce truth is sovereign.**
4. **Truth is expressed in the form of an affidavit.**
5. **An unrebutted affidavit, claim, or charge stands as truth in commerce.**
6. **An unrebutted affidavit becomes judgement in commerce.**
7. **A matter must be expressed to be resolved.**
8. **He who leaves the field of battle loses by default.**
9. **Sacrifice is the measure of credibility. One who has not been damaged by, given to, lost on account of, or put at risk by another has no basis to make claims or charges against another.**
10. **A lien or claim can be satisfied only through rebuttal by counter affidavit point-for-point, resolution by jury, or payment.**

caveat: — a Latin word meaning: *"let him beware."* A warning or emphasis for caution. It means, in other words, *that you are responsible for yourself and your own actions.* If you act on what you do not understand and cannot support in law, the consequences are entirely your responsibility.

caveat: — this synopsis does not constitute the practice of law or the giving of legal advice; *it is for informational purposes only.*

RPOI & RPII

In law, the ultimate or *supreme claimant* in a matter is called the *Real Party OF Interest* (RPOI); and its fictional representative (*its strawman*) is called the *Real Party IN Interest* (RPII).

The *Real Party IN Interest* speaks and acts for the *Real Party Of Interest.*

Today, the *Real Parties Of Interest* behind the bankruptcy of the United States and all law, are the agents and representatives of the U.S. government and the New World Order, who remain hidden from and unknown to the masses.

There are numerous terms used today to designate the RPOI that are largely interchangeable. These include but are not limited to: *"the bankers," "the government," "the system," "the elite," "the establishment," "the insiders,"* and the like. Individual people come and go; live, and die. The *actual* identities of the *Real Parties OF Interest* are irrelevant today. The important consideration is that the timeless and established laws of commerce now remain intact. The perceived *"villains"* are not the ultimate source of the problem. Those against whom we rail as being conspirators, arch-criminals, etc. are just filling in the void which we the people, through our *irresponsibility, ignorance, apathy, stupidity, and foolish trust,* have allowed to occur. In other words: **"We have met the enemy, and it is us!"** Both *cause and cure* reside in ourselves.

Law is Precise

Law revolves around how words are used and defined. *Deadly destructive force* is attached to the *words* and the *meanings* of the words that are used in legal documents and proceedings. To have any hope of knowing what you are doing in law and why, *it is essential* to know how the words then being used are defined. This is the key to what is happening today and what must be done. Understand the way the words are defined in law, and you can be clear and function on a firm footing. Fail to know what the words mean, and you can be damaged or even destroyed. An ancient maxim of law states:

In order rightly to comprehend a thing, inquire first into the names used; for a right knowledge of things depends upon their names.

Rules of Law

The rules of law are set forth in writing, syntax, grammar, etc. The way words are *legally defined* is the basis of the game. What the rules are, and their practical application and ramifications in the use of force today, is a function of *the legal definitions* of the words that have been used to write the rules. Words used in legal matters have *different meanings* than the same words in ordinary usage. Do not *assume* what words mean if your are not sure. In law, *assuming some point* can result in *slavery, imprisonment, or even death. "Those who expect to be both ignorant and free are expecting something that will never be."* — *Thomas Jefferson.*

There is no substitute for an excellent law dictionary, such as *Bouvier's, Ballentine's or Black's.* In any case, look up any legal term of which you are not certain. Do not take anything for granted. What you *do* know cannot hurt you because you can use your knowledge of the truth to "be set free." What you *do not know,* however, can get you killed. Ignorance is not bliss in law; it's potential suicide.

The Uniform Commercial Code

A *patriot* should acquire, if at all possible, a copy of the *Uniform Commercial Code* (UCC), since the UCC is *the supreme rule book* (*Bible*) of this world; other codes and bodies of law are all *subsets of,* and *subordinate* to the UCC. The *"common law"* of the planet is the commercial law that's embodied and codified in the UCC. *All other law* amounts to following rabbit trails and being endlessly mislead. Deal with the source — the UCC.

The Commercial Process

Notwithstanding the above *caveats,* commercial law and *the Commercial Process* are in many ways broad and like *normal law.* After all, the entire world functions by *the Commercial Process* set forth in the UCC. It is important to understand that *the Redemption-in-Law process* is fundamentally doable by anyone with normal intelligence. Our *disaster,* thus far, is having *done nothing,* due to ignorance, laziness, *and foolish trust in "authority."* It would be compounding folly to continue to do nothing because of fear. Understand the central points, become clear concerning *the foundation of the matter,* and build clearly and solidly from that point. Do not be afraid to ask for help. Once help is given, *verify the information* in the UCC, in law dictionaries, and with other people whom you believe have reason to know. Orderly, step by step progress is the means to obtaining complete legal security for you and yours.

The Real and Abstract

Everyone has to deal with *two fundamental aspects in life — the real and the abstract; the genuine and the artificial; the true and the false* — real being, aliveness and substance v. mental concepts, thoughts, ideas and beliefs.

The apparent duality of the real and the abstract, the tangible and the imaginary, is the difference between *the map* (*the symbol*) and *the territory* (*the land*) that it represents; the *name and the thing named;* the concept and the real. The *word "water"* is a symbol, an abstraction in thought; while *actual water* is tangible, real, and can quench one's thirst. One cannot drink the *word "water."*

Multiplicity of Abstractions

The human mind is capable of imagining unlimited varieties and configurations of *abstractions (images and concepts in thought).* These include non-tangible concepts, collections of concepts, and *mental constructs,* such as *"people," "nation," "corporation," "trust," "limited partnership,"* and *"government."* When an abstraction is *legally treated as real,* the result in law is a *fictitious entity.*

For instance, in law a *"person"* is not flesh and blood, but *an artificial construct in mind;* a fictitious *creature of law;* of contract; a *contractual device* representing a real being such as *"citizen," "driver,"* or *"officer."* Such an *artificial construct in mind* cannot be seen, touched, reasoned with, spoken to, or heard.

Since all law is contract, the *System* operates against you on the basis of the *presumption* that you have *contractually agreed* that your *"strawman"* — your name appearing in all capital letters; the name in which all industrial goods and services come to you — *is their (the System's) exclusive property.* Your *failure* to rebut their presumptions concerning you, *legally establishes* their presumptions in law as truth in commerce. (*See maxim #5 above*). By *failing to rebut* the state's *presumptive claims concerning you,* you *inadvertently* become the *exclusive property of the state,* in spite of the U.S. Constitution.

Fictitious entities can only deal with fictitious entities

Governments, under commercial law, can deal only with *fictitious entities,* such as *artificial persons (companies)* and the documents creating and representing them; such as birth certificates, certificates of title, corporations, trusts — and the contracts involving them. Such *persons* include your all-capital-letter name — *your artificial strawman.*

The *Real Parties OF Interest* who own the law and all the money that exists in the world today, and the agencies and resources of essentially all of the world's governments, created *your strawman* at the time of your birth. What they created and presume to own, they control. They can tax, regulate, and even *destroy* their "property" as they see fit, with no regard for constitutional restrictions and limitations.

The real you, your living, sentient, biological being, is as *indivisibly united* with your fictitious name, strawman, "person," as your ego is *inextricably united* with your body. Your strawman includes your ego and the words, concepts, thoughts, and ideas with which you interact with other people or *persons* in speaking or writing. That which is done to the strawman is *transferred ("transmitted")* to the living being linked thereto. A *strawman* is a *"transmitting utility."*

Rights & Power

The designers and operators of *the system* have very cleverly separated *your rights* from *your power* to sustain and enforce them. It is admitted that everyone possesses God-given, unalienable rights; but law is structured so that *unless you claim (redeem) your strawman via the Redemption-in-Law process,* you are bereft of power to *exer-*

cise those God-given rights. The government's admission that *you have rights,* while *closing you off* from power to *enforce* them, is a *hypocritical, fraudulent sham.* The practical result, *for all intents and purposes,* is that you have no rights at all — *unless and until you claim them.*

The Sovereign is King

A sovereign has the full right and power to use and dispense with his own property in any manner he wishes; as he sees proper and fit. *If the sovereign elite* — who own the strawman with which you are contractually presumed to have become unified — elect to tax, fine, regulate, enslave, or even *kill* your strawman, then you — *the physical, biological being* — experience the consequence in reality. In such a *legal status,* you are *devoid of capacity* to assert or enforce your rights. You have *no "standing in law."* A slave cannot take action against his master, who owns him.

Claim Ownership of Your Strawman

When you *take ownership* of your strawman, in accordance with *the lawful and legal procedures* required to do so, you *re-join* your inherent rights — rights which are innate, unalienable, and never leave you — with *the Certificate of Title (power)* to exercise and enjoy those rights. You then have a *total claim* on your strawman. You become the *Real Party OF Interest* in regard to your strawman; instead of the state. In such a case, *no other being* in the universe has any claim on your strawman. In such a case, *all other entities* are devoid of capacity to act against you or any property you have thusly secured. You are then the *"holder-in-due-course"* of your strawman.

Who Owns You Now?

The commercial crux of the matter is, WHO OWNS YOUR STRAWMAN AND YOU NOW? Unless *you* legally own your strawman, officials of *the system* possess the rights and power, *in law* (*of deadly force*) to treat you in any way *the system* mandates or allows, because *the system* owns *your strawman,* and basically, owns YOU!

On the other hand, if instead *YOU* own your strawman, no one in government or anywhere else, can *"state a claim upon which relief can be granted"* against you or your strawman — no one can penetrate your universe, *legally or commercially.* They are *estopped* (*barred; impeded; prevented; precluded*) *"ab initio"* (*from the beginning*).

Contractual Presumption

The system's presumption of *contractual ownership* of your strawman and you is the basis of *the system's* claim against you. When you *legally dissolve* the presumption of contract between you, and *the system's* ownership of your strawman and you, *the basis* of the government's claim on you is removed and you are *legally established* as sovereign and free.

Deny the error, and declare the truth. Empty the vessel, and fill it for your good.

12
Subjects Of The Crown

THE AMERICAN COLONIES were chartered through international financiers under the flag of the British Crown in England.

One hundred years *prior to the American War for Independence* in 1776 and the first fourth of July, the King's advisors warned him that the pastors in American churches were preaching Liberty and resistance to the King's restrictive confiscatory edicts, suggesting that the pastors be replaced with *regulated preachers* who would teach obedience to the Crown.

Certain international bankers who owned the Bank of England then, as they still do today, were using British forces under British rule to protect and control their large investments. Eventually, their oppression became too much to bear, so the American Colonists revolted and won their independence — or so they thought, and so we think today.

The battle cry heard up and down the coast was *"No king but King Jesus,"* and because of their powerful influence, American pastors were referred to as the *"Black Regiment."*

At the end of the war — when Gen. Cornwallis surrendered to Gen. Washington — Cornwallis prophesied this: *"A holy war will now begin on America, and when it is ended, America will be supposedly the Citadel of Freedom, — but her millions will unknowingly be loyal subjects of the Crown. Your churches will be used to teach the Jew's religion* (rejection of Jesus as the Messiah), *and in less than 200 years* (1781 + 200 = 1981) *the whole nation will be working for World Government."*

From its beginning, agents of the bankers sought to infiltrate and re-form the Colonial Government and retain control of America's vast wealth, her resources and our labor — even if the Colonials *had not been upset* with British rule. The only way that they could accomplish this was by gaining control of America's economic system — so this is what they did.

After *fomenting* the War for Independence in 1776, and the Civil War in 1860 — in a effort to divide America and prosper on the chaos and bloodshed of war — the agents of the bankers and their allies prevailed. Finally, on December 29, 1913, when most of Congress was home for the holidays, the Federal Reserve Act was rammed through, and enacted and signed into law by President Woodrow Wilson.

This Act took the monetary powers away from the people, through their representatives, under Article I, Section 8, Clause 5 of the U.S. Constitution, and placed it into the hands of the very same banking families, through their private monopoly deceptively called the "Federal Reserve System." It is not federal, it has no reserves, it pays no income taxes, it has never been audited, and it *creates fiat money out of nothing* by paying the U.S. Treasury a few cents apiece to print "Federal Reserve Notes" (*evidences of debt*) (*regardless of denomination*) that it then loans into existence at full face value, plus interest, which is usury.

These bankers thrive upon strife, contention, destruction and war. They covertly promote unrest throughout the world — for their profit — at the expense of innocent misery, suffering and blood. It took them just 4 years to foment and get America involved in World War One, and just 20 years to bankrupt the U.S. Federal Government (1913-1933).

World Wars I & II, and all wars since, were fomented by these predators. Their political prostitute — Franklin Delano Roosevelt — implemented Cornwallis' prophecy. The bankers deliberately orchestrated the economic collapse of 1929 — the Great Depression — placing Americans in a state of economic servitude.

Roosevelt's *first attempt* at invoking the *socialist scheme* failed because the U.S. Supreme Court struck it down, as unconstitutional. (*Railroad Retirement Board v. Alton Railroad Company, May 6, 1935.*) So he packed the Supreme Court with friends who would thereafter cooperate with his plans.

Congress has no authority to legislate for the social welfare of the worker, and the Constitution forbids the direct taxation of Americans who live within the 50 Union States. (*Article I, Section 2, Clause 3, and Article 1, Section 9, Clause 4, USC*).

Roosevelt and his agents bypassed the Constitution by invoking the Social Security Act three months later, on August 14, 1935, *as a foreign-treaty-based law.*

Under the Constitution, the President has the authority to enter into treaties with foreign countries and have them ratified by the Senate. The Supreme Court could not object to *the treaty-based legislation* that taxed American citizens in their own country when *they volunteered* to apply for government benefits that are provided *under foreign treaty law.*

Due to the deliberately orchestrated economic strife, millions of Americans — in ignorance and desperation — accepted Roosevelt's offer of a *New Deal* and Roosevelt *as their Savior,* and *voluntarily* enslaved themselves and their posterity in a perpetual *heavy yoke of bondage,* by applying for and obtaining, and using a Social Security

Number (SSN). By doing so, the people became the registered subjects of the state.

And which foreign country is Roosevelt's *treaty-based law* with? You guessed it. It's with the United Kingdom — Great Britain. Since then, Social Security has become a general sign of obedience to the State. Everyone erroneously believes that the law requires them to have a SSN, when in truth, *it is voluntary.*

In essence, this SSN has become the *de facto* I.D. of all Americans who are now — unknowingly — subjects of the British Crown. Americans are considered to be a *"human resource" — assets; feudal serfs* — belonging to the international bankers, because of the bankruptcy of the United States, Inc.

"Ye are bought with a price; be not ye the servants of men." — *I Corinthians 7:23.*

13
The New Word Order - Or Release

"Choose ye this day whom ye will serve..." (Joshua 24:15).

The Biblical regathering of Israel began in America in 1776. It involved three consecutive 70 year periods of servitude to the world because of our Founding Father's pledge of America's assets to our creditors in Europe.

By mortgaging God's people to their creditors in Europe, they rejected God as their ruler and king — once again.

Even so, we can set ourselves free from America's debt to the kings of Europe, on an individual basis. Why? Because we've reached the crossroads of three periods of bondage to the kings of this world.

To drive the British troops off American soil, and to keep itself afloat, the Confederate States borrowed money from the English Crown, and when the Paris Peace treaty was signed in 1783, eighteen loans were extended for another six years.

When Congress realized that they were not going to be able to pay back the loans, when they became due in 1789, they convened a Constitutional Convention in 1787 to establish a "constitutum."

CONSTITUTUM: "an agreement to pay ones own or another's existing debt." (Blacks Law 7th, page 307).

CONSTITUTOR: "a person who, by agreement, become responsible for the payment of another's debt." (ibid).

To resolve their dilemma, Congress had the states assume its existing debt to the Crown, and it's been doing this, ever since that time.

The government that had originally signed for the loans made the states its co-sureties (co-signers), as Junior pleads with his parents to co-sign for him so the bank will not repossess his car.

The real purpose of the Constitution was to give the Crown in England a mortgage on the supposedly freed, new states.

The states mortgaged their future, via the Constitution, in 1789. They sold their inheritance for a mess of pottage, and incurred a 70 year penalty for their failure to pay the debt.

1.   The first seventy-year period takes us to the first "Year of release" in 1859, and the Civil War. The Civil War prepared the people for the government takeover of the States, that had become accommodation parties for its debts.

2. The second seventy-year period takes us to the second "Year of release" in 1929, and the Great Depression.

The Great Depression prepared the people for the socialization of the nation. When the ongoing mortgage was called in 1933, the states had no assets (they were bankrupt as well), so Congress had the people pledge their private assets to the public domain so the public could borrow funds to support itself and make payments on its loans.

3. The third seventy-year period takes us to the third "Year of release", 1999, and the Clinton impeachment trial. The Clinton impeachment trial was a national referendum for the nation to decide if it wanted to come out from under the 210 year mortgage or remain in bankruptcy to the Crown and proceed with the New World Order established in 1933.

The nation chose to stay in slavery to the national debt so it's playing out its part in the one world-government of today.

The Law of Servitude (re: master and slave) applied to that ""Year of release"," 1999, when the servant was set free. But if the servant loved his master, and desired to continue in servitude to him, he could enter voluntary servitude again (Exodus 21:2-6). So the United States volunteered to be a servant of the Crown once again.

But the Congress had to give each individual member of the U.S. Corporation the opportunity to "come out from among them, and be separate," and be no longer liable for the nation and its ever-increasing national debt.

The people can choose, individually, to "come out from among them and be separate," and be responsible for themselves.

"Come out from among them, and be ye separate, and touch not the unclean thing . . ." (2 Corinthians 6:17).

14
Regain Your Standing In Law

capacity: — *ability; qualification; legal power or right.*

REGAIN the legal *"capacity"* (*key word*) of a sovereign, and you have *standing in law* to enforce your rights, and can successfully rebut the presumptions of law by which the entire legal system functions. The presumption of law is that — *as a free will sovereign exercising your power of free will and choice* — you have knowingly, intentionally, and voluntarily contracted to be bound with and thereby subject *to the system.* If you can properly rebut that *presumption of bondage* you become free. If you fail to do so, your failure is *a legal default* (*agreement by silence*) signifying agreement with the position of *the system* — that you are indeed a slave.

Self-enforcing Rules
The rules of commercial law are *self-enforcing.* The law is *self-supporting.* If you use the law *improperly* (*which includes failure to use it at all*) you lose in any controversy by default. If you use the rules *properly,* you not only win, but place the entirety of the law-enforcement machinery of the world on your side, instead of against you.

Historical Review
The landmark Supreme Court case of 1795 — *Penhallow vs. Doane's Administrators,* — defines governments succinctly *as corporations.*

Inasmuch as every government is a corporation, *an artificial person* (*an abstraction or a creature of the mind*), it can only deal with *other artificial persons. The imaginary* — having no reality or substance — cannot create or attain parity with *the real.*

The legal aspect of this is that no government, or any law, agency, aspect, or court thereof, can concern itself with anything other than *corporate artificial persons* and the contracts between them.

One might immediately dispute this statement by pointing out that people are acted upon by government officials every day. The reason this can occur in law is because the *powers-that-be* who know and use the law to their advantage, *have stolen, conquered, subjugated, and laid claim* to the planet and the six billion people on it, by applying this foundational and inviolable axiom of law:

An UNREBUTTED affidavit, claim, or charge (*no matter how preposterous, criminal, or illegitimate*) **stands as truth in commerce."** (*Maxim #5, page 87*).

The above maxim is true of necessity, because unless what is asserted is rebutted or disputed by the affected party, there is no basis for anyone to know or act in any manner contrary to the unrebutted and undisputed claim or charge.

This is a free-will universe. The *unit* of experience, rights, and sovereignty is each particular man or woman. No one can speak for you other than you — including rebutting or disputing a presumption. No one but you can know your own truth or has any authority to assert it. This is the basis of the ancient maxim of law:

He who fails to assert his rights has none.

The government acts against the *artificial person* (*your strawman*) which it creates and owns. You are thereby acted upon because of the *government's presumption* that you have knowingly, intentionally, and voluntarily contracted to be unified with or identified with the *artificial person* (*your strawman*) owned by the *Real Party OF Interest* (RPOI) for whom the government corporation fronts as the *Real Party IN Interest* (RPII). If you do not rebut the presumption, it stands as truth and judgment in commerce and the law.

The System's contract of ownership of your strawman and you is considered to be valid because you failed to dispute the *presumed contract* — and agreed to it by your silence — so you lose by default. Or worse yet, you *expressly ratified* the contract by actions of written assent. To accept *any benefit* from *the system* — *without rebutting the system's presumption of ownership of your strawman* — is to contractually incur the obligations associated therewith.

Implied Ratification

Ratification by *implied contract* occurs when you order and consume a meal in a restaurant. You have by your actions, and without signing a written contract, contractually agreed to pay for the meal.

Express Ratification

Ratification by *express contract* occurs whenever you sign a form or *an application* to accept any benefit or privilege — such as to drive a car; for welfare or food stamps; for unemployment compensation, etc. One who *accepts the contracted benefit* incurs the *contractual obligations* attached to it.

In the case of contracts with the government, the obligations you incur are wholly decided beforehand by the government. Such a wholesale contract with the government is called an *"adhesion contract."* It is structured and enforced per the discretion of *the stronger party* which in this case is *the government.* A citizen contracts to buy *a bill of goods* subject to the government's *dictating the goods.*

The basic contracted instrument and how to eliminate its claim on you

All human interaction, commerce, and law, is contract, because all the official actions of the agents of government, without exception, arise from their presumption that they have an express, implied, presumed and existing contract with you. The key issues of which pertain to the following questions:

1. What is the ultimate, central core, contractual instrument embodying a certificate of title to yourself and your body, labor, and property, whereby the holder of said instrument may be deemed in law to hold title to your strawman?

2. By what means in law can any presumed contract of ownership of your strawman (*by the System*) be effectively rebutted, disputed, and rendered null and void?

3. How can you become the sovereign owner, the "holder-in-due-course" (HDC) of your strawman and the above-reference instrument? A "holder-in-due-course" of something is the only one who holds a valid claim to that something; the ultimate owner of that something.

4. What is your capacity and "standing in law" if you *fail* to established yourself as the owner of your strawman and his certificate of title?

5. What is your capacity and "standing in law" when you *do* establish yourself as the owner of your strawman and his certificate of title?

To answer the *first question,* the certificate of title to your being, rights, faculties, labor, and property, in perpetuity, is *your birth certificate.* Your birth certificate is the *Certificate of Title* to your strawman. It is essentially, a *certificate, or deed* to yourself. Literally and legally, it is a *warehouse receipt,* a Bill of Lading, FOB (*Free On Board*) the hospital of your birth.

Ever since the Declaration of Independence of 1776, the *world powers — kings, popes, money changers, the elite* — have operated unceasingly to obtain full control, ownership, and subjugation of the American people and the USA. To date, *they have succeeded in great measure.* The weakness of their scheme is that it has been founded on *deceit and rebuttable, or disputable presumptions,* and it will not stand the test of genuine scrutiny, the full light of day.

The entire operation dissolves when *the presumption* on which it functions is correctly rebutted; which rebuttal is the purpose of the *Redemption-in-Law procedure.* The strength of its position is that the American people, *in particular,* and the people of the world, *in general* — living in ignorance and apathy — have unknowingly *given away* their freedom and thereby defaulted themselves into slavery.

Since *all law is contract,* the would-be rulers-of-the-world have *"succeeded"* to its rule by making us, by contract, subject to them.

However: ***"As a thing is bound, so it is unbound."*** In other words, the same rules that made us slaves can make us free again when and if properly applied. ***"The rules, are the rules, are the rules."*** Deny the error, and declare the truth. The legal consequences concerning our lives are exclusively a function of *our proper use of the rules* that exist.

Increasing numbers of people are becoming aware that *the contract* embodying the presumed nexus between a man and the government that rules him, *is structurally defective.* In order for a contract to be valid — *to be a contract at all* — it must include specific essentials.

Fundamentally, a contract is the embodiment and codification of *an agreement.* In order to achieve an agreement, all parties must understand the full scope and nature — the full terms and conditions — of the proposed contract, *or no agreement, and hence no contract,* exists. Parties must arrive at a *"meeting of the minds"* for any agreement to exist. People enter into contracts in order to better their position. No one enters into a contract to be diminished, cheated, or destroyed. *Any purported* contract that fails to be characterized *by mutual good faith, a meeting of the minds, and open and full disclosure of all terms and conditions,* is either void, or voidable. It is flawed from inception and it can be rendered null and void by the election of the deceived or defrauded party.

It is *essential* to the existence of a contract that there be parties *capable of contracting* (*capacity*), that there be *knowledgeable consent* (*a meeting of the minds*), and that there be a lawful objective and sufficient cause, or consideration. All persons may contract, except minors, persons of unsound mind, and persons deprived of civil rights.

The consent of the parties to a contract must be *freely given, mutually expressed, and communicated* by each other to each other.

Apparent consent is not valid when obtained 1) through *duress,* 2) through *menace,* 3) through *fraud,* 4) through *undue influence,* 5) *lack of cause or consideration,* or 6) through *mistake.*

The crucial and incurable flaw in all government, and the *"laws"* which issue therefrom, is the non-existence of *genuine agreement* between the parties due to *absence of full disclosure, a true meeting of the minds, and mutual good faith.* In presuming to have formed a bona fide good faith contract with its citizens, the government *never informed them* of the full terms and conditions of the contract. Citizens *were never told* that they would be sacrificing their freedom and autonomy, and that they were agreeing to become the ruled and exploited slaves of whoever occupy positions of *"authority"* in the so-called *"government."* This situation exists because we-the-people have deluded ourselves, lied to ourselves; and failed to communicate and be sincere with ourselves. The *outer world* of law and government is the effect of what we-the-people have *inwardly* caused or allowed. We should not blame the messenger for the message.

According to the timeless and universal principles of *contract law,* no contract exists in the absence of *genuine agreement.* At best there can be only a *contractual presumption* based on the deceived party having been kept in the dark, ignorant of the truth; or having foolishly trusted the other party. When one fails to *object to, or rebut* the presumption that a contract exists, it may be rightfully *assumed or legally construed* that indeed a contract truly *does* exist.

Although *fraud is always unlawful, fraud is not illegal* in state rulership systems. The rationale for this is that *one may assent to fraud.* More seriously, all governments are necessarily, structurally and inherently fraudulent, and cannot be otherwise. It is therefore self-evident that *fraud must be legal* in order for a government to be able to self-adjudicate itself as legal to exist. In other words, *to assent to the existence of a government, is to assent to the legality of fraud.*

In law, there is a difference between *"assent"* and *"consent."* One may *"assent"* to fraud by government by *non-rebuttal (silence).* One cannot *"consent"* to fraud, however, because *"consent"* requires actual agreement — a meeting of the minds, full disclosure, and good faith.

In law a government is defined, *"inter alia"* (among other things) as *a constructive trust.* A *constructive trust* is a mixture of *law and fraud.* The law may be valid, but *the fraud* is that *some men (sovereigns)* possess a *higher claim, right, or title* to universal law than *other men,* but — *through ignorance* — they do not claim it.

The cardinal point, on the basis of which the *powers-that-be* have stolen and enslaved the world, is:

An unrebutted affidavit, claim, or charge stands as truth in commerce. — *Maxim #5.*

Another maxim of commercial law is that:

A matter must be expressed to be resolved. — *Maxim #7.*

Only each unique, autonomous being has the knowledge, right, or duty *to affirm his truth.* No one else can do it for him; or is even obliged to try. In fact, doing so *is unlawful,* inasmuch as *only a man himself, can speak for himself.*

The Holder-in-due-Course

In commercial law the *ultimate owner* of an instrument is called the *"holder-in-due-course"* (HDC) — the only one who possesses a valid claim. A mere *"holder"* may legally possess the instrument, but lacks the *ultimate claim* held by the *"holder-in-due-course."* To be the HDC requires that the *"holder"* accept it for value in good faith, without notice of any claim or defense against it, and that he can enforce his holding of the instrument, free from all claims and personal defenses.

A *"holder"* does not become a *"Holder-in-due-Course"* of an instrument by purchasing it as part of a bulk transaction that is not in the regular course of the business of the transferor.

As stated earlier in this *ongoing synopsis,* your birth certificate is a *warehouse receipt.* Birth certificates are bundled together and transferred, or purchased and sold, in bulk. Moreover, this purchase and transfer is *"not in the regular course of business of the transferor"* — who is YOU!

In addition, possession was not taken *"in mutual good faith"* and the *"holder"* cannot enforce the instrument free from all claims and personal defenses. This means that whoever acts *as if he owned* your Birth Certificate can only be a *"holder"* of it — never the actual *"holder-in-due-course."*

The HDC is the *most powerful position* in any exchange! When you understand and apply this fact, your whole life changes. You are *sovereign and untouchable* with respect to anything of which you are the HDC. Why not be the HDC of yourself, of all of your affairs, and of everything else concerning which you wish to be the actual owner?

A profound situation

This entire matter is profound. Just as *all manifest existence is created by thought,* all our thoughts, and words too, create. All that we are and everything we experience is created by thought. ***"In the beginning was the Word."***

Be careful what you wish for; you just might get it. — ***"As ye sow, so shall ye reap."***

Since *everything we experience is the product of thought,* what value inheres in fighting, resisting, running, or hiding from the natural-law effects of what we ourselves have allowed? *"Peter, put up thy sword."* — *John 18:11.* No one can escape from himself. Man's fundamental problem is that he deals with effects, while ignoring the cause. A major reason for this is the apparent interval of time between cause and effect. Birth is not instantaneous with conception; harvest does not occur at the instant the seed is planted. Intermediate, natural law processes are vast — and inexorable.

Our entire legal situation is the playing out of the laws of existence.

When the Bible states: *"Seek ye first the Kingdom of God, and all these things shall be added unto you"* (Matthew 6:33) it is stating, *in devotional or theological terms,* what is stated by Lao-Tzu *in existential terms:*

"The source of life is as a mother. Be fond of both mother (source) and child (creation) but know the mother dearer, and you outlive death. Curb your tongue and senses, and you are beyond trouble; loose them and you are beyond help."

"Blessed are the meek, for they shall inherit the earth." — *Jesus at Matthew 5:5.*

Commercially, every word uttered is *a commercial presentment;* a contractual act — an *offer or acceptance* to be either *accepted or rejected.* When in court, and the judge asks an off-point question or makes an off-point demand, and you innocently answer or comply, you have *inadvertently, but nevertheless profoundly, formed a contract with* him and granted him jurisdiction over you and your straw-man — a potentially disastrous move. Not knowing how to deal with such trickery can land you in jail.

The point is that, *"normal life"* consists of attempts to acquire — by grant, theft, grasping, physical labor, or some other external effort — *ownership (title)* of a manifest thing (*the outward expression of a inner, unmanifest desire*). This is being fond of *the child (effect)* instead of *the mother (cause).* We can truly *own* something only when we are one with what we desire at its source — *the Kingdom of God or Origin of life* — the true reality and unmanifest source of our manifest selves.

If we act *"out there"* in the realm of some phase of the vast set of seemingly natural law processes which mechanically and heartlessly (*like the Tin Man of Oz*) carry out *"cause and effect,"* we can never truly fulfill our desire. This is falling for, or becoming absorbed in, *the Wizard's light show,* which is a *chimera* (*a vain or idle fancy*) alien to us.

The key to becoming the *"holder-in-due-course"* is *"Acceptance for Value."*

The fact that your birth certificate is held *in limbo* by parties who can never be the HDC of it means that your birth certificate is *in suspension,* waiting for you to redeem it.

"Redemption" has been defined (*in part*) as:

"Deliverance from the power of alien domination, and the enjoyment of the resulting freedom that it entails. It involves the idea of restoration to one who possesses a more fundamental and higher right or interest."

You achieve union of *"effect" and "cause"* simply *by ac-*

cepting that which already belongs to you — and the dominion that goes with it.

Only you and you alone can become the HDC, and the fact that you do, *is the evidence* of your exchange for value. This completes the cycle and makes you the owner and *"holder-in-due course"* of the entire matter. Such an action *redeems* your strawman from *"alien"* control.

When an *offer* is made, title passes upon *acceptance* of the offer. This meeting of the minds constitutes *agreement* — a finalized contract. All that remains is to give *evidence* of the exchange in the form of a *bill of exchange.* Under the *current law,* however (*the Federal Truth in Lending Act*) a borrower may change his mind and *withdraw* his or her offer within a 72 hour period of grace, *without* penalty.

The *Department of Commerce* accepted your *Birth Record* from your mother, who unwittingly pledged you to the state, and thereby delivered you into bondage, slavery, and the status of being *chattel property* in permanently indentured servitude to the state.

The *Department of Commerce* became the *"de facto"* (*in fact*) *"holder"* of the Certificate of Rights to you and your body, labor, and property, giving you a *"claim check"* (*your birth certificate*) in return. Whoever the *"holder"* of your birth certificate is; he has no more right to it than someone holding a possession of yours in your absence, waiting for you to return and claim it — *to redeem what is your own.*

The current *"holder"* of your birth certificate is able to capitalize on it, *in your stead,* due to your inaction and silence, because of your failure to instruct the *"holder"* otherwise. *"While the cat's away, the mice will play."*

When you, *as king,* abnegate your throne to your underlings, they run amuck. When you *reclaim ownership* of your birth certificate, by *accepting it for value,* you regain your crown — you *re-install* yourself on your throne. You *re-gain* dominion and sovereignty over your own kingdom. The Wizard (*the alleged Real Party OF Interest pretender to your throne*) and all your *servants* (*government bureaucrats*) are banished from power.

You cannot obtain this condition by earning it, fighting for it, or running for it. No one but you can give you back your throne. *Arguing or fighting back equals assenting.* The only issue after assenting is, *"What's the penalty?"* No one can ever attain commercial freedom by *fighting* for it. Attempting to do so is futile. *Freedom is already yours.* Freedom must only be claimed.

There are *only two classes* of people in the world and in any legal proceeding: *creditors* and *debtors.*

When your sovereignty is established in law you become the *creditor,* and any adverse party becomes the *debtor* in any dispute with you. If you neglect to establish your *sovereignty in law,* you do not *own* yourself and you have no legal capacity — you are devoid of *standing* to assert any of your rights. You remain a *permanent debtor* and must always lose in any dispute with the *system* for *"failing to state a claim upon which relief can be granted."*

Re-claiming *ownership of your strawman* acts as an estoppel, or bar, to any and all people who come against you. If you do not *reclaim* your right to the title of your strawman by filing a *UCC Lien* against it, thereby making you the *creditor* and *absolute ruler* of your strawman, you are not sovereign and you will *lose* in the resolution of any dispute. This is why, if you contemplate hiring an attorney to represent you in any legal defense against *the system,* ask him if he can make you the *"holder-in-due-course"* of the action. If he cannot (*which he cannot*) then you will *lose.* The best any attorney can do is *make a deal,* which is a *compromise* (*how much?*) rather than *a clear win.* You must be the *"holder-in-due-course"* (HDC) of you strawman to be able to ensure victory at law.

Deny the error and declare the truth. Empty the vessel and fill it for your good.

"Blessed are the peacemakers: for they shall be called the children of God." — *Jesus at Matthew 5:9.*

15

On Condition Of Proof Of Claim

TRUTH is stranger than fiction.

From analysis of the Redemption Process — it seems that the Governor of each state holds the *commercial indemnity bond* for each *unincorporated limited liability company* (*unincorporated means "strawman"*) in "this state" (*i.e. each state corporation*).

When a Redemptor asks the question in court, *"Are you holding the bond on this issue?"* — if the bond is not produced at that time *or within 72 hours of the inquiry or demand,* this default creates an estoppel against the Governor and his *"agents provocateur"* (*the court officials*) from ever *"charging"* the account against the *unincorporated strawman,* that otherwise would result in liability to the *man.*

If the bond were presented to the Redemptor it could be *conditionally accepted* — (*endorsed on its face and dated*) — and this *acceptance* would cancel the liability to the named beneficiary — *the real man.*

If the official (*or any other presenter*) refuses to produce the bond, then the debt, duty and liability that gives rise to the obligation is cancelled — otherwise the Securities and Exchange Commission (SEC) would have to get involved.

Conditional Acceptance For Value

"Acceptance for Value" of a claim by the private natural man, *Nomen, Pronorneu, Cognomenation,* must be on the condition that the presenter provides "Proof of Claim." This he will not and cannot do.

"Proof of Claim" is the act and statute that grants power

to a state legislature (1) *to create* the new *de facto* federal corporate form of government that now functions, (2) *to function* in that federal corporate form, and (3) *to function* in a *federal territorial* capacity.

"Proof of Claim" is the act and statute that creates the *de facto* state government federal corporate form that (4) functions in a federal territorial capacity, and (5) evades Article I, Section 10 of the Constitution of the United States of America wherein it states that *"No State shall make anything but gold and silver coin a tender a payment of debts,"* explicitly retaining all rights as to capacity, use, place and law form, "without prejudice."

"**without prejudice**" means "without loss of any right;" in a way that does not harm or cancel the legal rights or privileges of a party.

16
Redemption And The Lord's Release

Our War for independence from Great Britain began 1776 and ended with the Treaty of Peace in Paris in 1783.

To finance the War for Independence from the King of England, the thirteen American colonies borrowed money from the Crown of England; 3,000,000 livres in 1778; 1,000,000 livres in 1779; 4,000,000 livres in 1780; and 6,000,000 livres in 1782; or 18,000,000 (18 million) livres in all.

On July 16, 1782, Benjamin Franklin, Esq. signed a treaty with the King of France — a mortgage loan agreement under international law — establishing 1) a creditor, 2) a debtor, 3) consideration, 4) specific performance on the debt, and 5) the opportunity for others (such as yourself) to contribute to paying on the loan (hence your involvement in the debt).

The loan was for six years, due and payable on the January 1, 1789, and the Continental Congress defaulted on the loan. This default placed the new nation into bankruptcy to the Crown of England.

The reason for the constitutional convention, and forming an American Constitution, at that time, was to amend the Articles of Confederation to incorporate the obligation of this loan. The signing of the Constitution in 1789, after the default on the loan, was *a disguised bankruptcy* of the United States to satisfy the creditor, the Crown of England.

CONSTITUTOR: A person who, by agreement, becomes responsible for the payment of another's debt. — Blacks Law Dictionary, 7th edition, p.307.

The first National Bank of the United States was established, two years later in 1791, by George Washington, under emergency law rule, as a private bank to provide securities of the bankrupt United States, for the Crown in England.

When the bank's 20 year charter expired in 1811 it was not renewed. So England used its military force during the War of 1812-1814 to attack the United States and burn the Capital Building and the White House, in order to destroy the original 13th Amendment, and have the Crown's securities restored under international law.

The second National Bank of the United States was established, two years later in 1816, to continue to provide the securities to the Crown of England for Congress' defaulted loan.

The principles of international law are dictated by international public law and the law of nations. One interesting aspect of the law of nations is the law that deals with bondage, captivity, redemption, and release.

"At the end of every seven years thou shalt make a release. Every creditor that lendeth ought unto his neighbor shall release it. Because it is called the Lord's release." — Deuteronomy 15:1,2.

"And these nations shall serve the king of Babylon seventy years." — Jeremiah 25:11.

The Lord's release for man is after every 7 years, and for nations it is after 10 times 7 years, or 70 years.

For instance: The Captivity of the Judaites in Babylon lasted for 70 years, from 607 B.C. to 537 B.C.

Jacob served his father-in-law Laban for 21 years. He served 7 years as an apprentice, 7 years as a dowry for his wife Leah, and 7 years as a dowry for his wife Rachel — a total of 21 years. After 21 years his time was his own. After 21 years Jacob was set free from his economic contract with his father-in-law. This 21 year period is known as "the time of Jacob's Trouble."

Captivity for man is 7 years, and for nations, 10 times 7 years, or 70 years.

There is a short Captivity — such as the 70 year captivity of the Judaites of Daniel's time in Babylon, and the 70 year captivity of the Soviet Union as a communist nation in our time — and a long captivity — such as the 210 year captivity of God's People in Egypt, in Moses time, prior to the Exodus.

The greater Captivity for man is 21 years (3x21=70) and the greater Captivity for nations is 10 times 21 years or 210 years. The Children of Israel were subject to Egypt for 210 years, before God set them free through Moses.

The United States went into captivity under international economic law for 210 years, just as the Children of Israel did under Egypt in Moses' time.

When we add 210 years to the first loan default date of January 1, 1789, we get January 1, 1999 — the year of release for the American colonies, under international law, from the bankruptcy of the United States that resulted from Congress' loans of 1789.

When dealing in bankruptcy, an individual can go through bankruptcy and have his debts declared "discharged," and then turn around and *renew his obligation* for the debt by an operation of law. The law will then require that the person pay the discharged debt even though it had been discharged in the bankruptcy.

This procedure was used in 1999 to get the American people to renew the corporate debt of the United States to the Crown of England, during its time of release from that debt under international law. The second 13th Amendment to the Constitution permits "voluntary servitude" — and Exodus 21:5 allows a servant to voluntarily serve his master after his release in the "Year of Release."

Most of our legislators in Washington, D.C. are Esquire attorneys who work for the Crown of England — whether they know it or not.

Let's assume that they know that the United States is in Chapter 11 bankruptcy to the Crown of England (or its principals), and that the year of the Lord's Release is up so that the United States can elect to have its national debt discharged and its sovereign status as a republic restored, instead of being the democracy it now is.

This means that the tax collections, for the past 70 years, to pay back the debt to the Crown, would expire — unless the United States renewed its debt to the Crown.

Let's assume that the attorney/politicians did not want to tell the people that an option to stop paying on the national debt to the Crown existed in this "Year of release." However, under international law, both parties must be informed of their options, if their agreement is to be altered or renewed.

Under international law, the Crown of England and its agents had to inform the American people of the law that entitled them to be released from the nation's debt to the Crown and be free.

Thence the question: How could the Crown of England, and its esquire agents in D.C., tell us that the United States could elect to have its national debt discharged in the "Year of Release," 1999, in such a way that we would not catch on to that fact?

Let's assume that the attorneys of the Crown (and its principals including the Vatican) establish a **"great debate"** to decide whether or not the people of the United States want to leave their servitude and be free.

Let's assume that the **"great debate"** will be such that no living soul in the land could escape the debate and its conclusive decision. All must know about it. It must be the talk of the town throughout the land. It must involve great principles at the highest level of the law.

Let's assume that the vehicle chosen for the debate would distract the American people from the true intent and meaning of the debate. What kind of a **"great debate"** would we, as agents of the Crown, choose? I know!

Let's charge the U.S. President with a crime!

Of course, we're not really interested in what the president might do to commit the crime; the real issue would be the procedure that we would use to bring this issue before the American people.

The attorney/politicians would pretend that they know not what procedure they should use. They would refer that question to the American people, as to what to do in a criminal presidential trial.

Under what law form (venue) is the president to be tried?

If the president is accused of some criminal offense, then he must be tried by some form of tribunal, but which one? The nation has been a *military democracy* for many years. A democracy is a military government that is ruled in an emergency by a Commander-in-Chief. In a democracy the people are not free. They are the subjects of a *democratic law form.*

If a nation wants to be released from captivity, it must revert from a *military democracy,* back to a *republic at peace,* and leave its commercial bondage behind.

The people should have insisted that the rules of the Clinton Impeachment trial be set *in the republic law form* of a sovereign nation, under the original Constitution FOR the United States of 1789. Under *a republican law form* a president can be impeached.

If the nation wants to renew its debt to the international bankers and the Crown, after the "Year of Release," it must continue under a democratic law form under which the Commander-in-Chief is sovereign and cannot be touched by the people under his charge.

The people should have insisted that the rules of the Clinton Impeachment trial be set, *not in the democratic law form of a military nation but* under the de facto Constitution OF the United States of 1891. Because under a democratic law form the commander-in-chief can never be impeached, because his rule is law; he can only be sanctioned in his public capacity as president.

The American people were being asked to vote, *by a national referendum,* on whether the nation was to become free or continue as subjects to the king and the international bankers who are foreign to the United States. The notion that President Clinton had committed a crime was the vehicle for the debate, not its subject.

Since there was *no lawful "Notice of Protest,"* the old law form remained in effect. Since there was *no lawful "Notice of Protest"* before the Senate voted for the democracy and against impeachment, the law form of the bankruptcy, and our debtor enslavement to the English Crown continued in force.

"Now these are the judgments that thou shalt set before them. If thou buy an Hebrew servant (this is what happened when we were sold into bankruptcy)*, six years shall he serve: and in the seventh he shall go out free for nothing* (this was the national release in the seventh year), *[but] if the servant shall plainly say, "I love my master. . . I will not go out free: Then his master shall bring him unto the judges* (this was the result of the "great debate")*; he shall also bring him to the door, or unto the door post; and his master shall bore his ear through with an aul; and he shall serve him for ever."* — *Exodus 21:1,2,5.*

The practice of placing an earring in an ear is the practice of branding one as a slave to his master under voluntary consent. Hence the significance of an earring in the ear. **The symbol of the slave.**

The William Jefferson Clinton Impeachment Trial was about voluntary consent. It had nothing to do with the accusations involved. It had nothing to do with whether he was guilty or not. It dealt with *the "rules of procedure"* upon which the trial was to be conducted. By not choosing the rules of a republic, we chose the law form for the triers of the case. We chose the debtor law form, and kept the democracy in force. We said, "We will not go free."

There has never been a real impeachment process of any President of the United States since our nation was founded, because the United States has been under bankruptcy to the Crown of England since the Revolutionary War.

We are in breach of an international treaty when we trade with the Crown's corporate holdings in the United States. By engaging in the King's Commerce in this way, we are *"converting to our own use"* assets of the British Crown, resulting in the Crown's rulership over us. We are being held accountable for a loan that came due more than 200 years ago in 1789.

The creditor is the head, and the debtor is the tail. The United States has still been a British Colony since that time. Wake up, America. It's always darkest before the dawn. Even though the bankruptcy of the United States has been renewed, you can still individually have your part in *the forgiveness of the national debt* as a result of the Lord's Release, through the Redemption in Law process, per HJR-192 and UCC 3-419.

EPILOGUE:

After the depression of 1908, the United States negotiated with the international bankers, *to which its debt was again in default;* at J.P. Morgan's vacation retreat, at Jekyll Island, Georgia, in the fall of 1910. The United States received a 20 year moratorium on paying its debt to the Crown in exchange for its promise to permit the establishment of *a third private, central bank* (the Federal Reserve) in which the securities of the nation would be deposited as sureties on its unpaid debt.

Twenty years later, the United States defaulted on its loans again. This default resulted from the stock market collapse of 1929, and the United States was reorganized again under chapter 11 bankruptcy, putting its citizens again under the unpaid debt that made them, once again, captive servants of the Crown.

The citizens of the United States went into captivity under international economic law like the Children of Israel in Jeremiah's time.

17
Know Then Who You Are

IN ORDER to comprehend a thing, inquire first into the name, for a right knowledge of things depends upon their names.

"Good name in man or woman, dear my lord,
is the immediate jewel of their soul:
Who steals my purse, steals trash;
tis something, nothing; 'Twas mine, 'tis his,
and has been slave to thousands;
But he that filches from me my good name
Robs me of that which not enriches him,
and makes me poor indeed."

Othello, the Moor of Venice,
Act III, Scene 3,
by William Shakespeare.

JOHN J. DOE is not the same as John James Doe. JOHN J. DOE is a *fiction* and John James Doe is the name of a *real man.* John James is his *given* name and his *family* name is Doe.

Look at your drivers license and see to whom it really belongs. It is issued to your fictional strawman. Check your utility bill . . . it too is issued to your fictional strawman, not to you.

The *first* name mentioned, JOHN J. DOE, is written in all-capital letters. It is a fictional *front man* acting in behalf of John James Doe. The *real* name, John James Doe, is written in cursive — caps and lower-case letters. The *first* name, JOHN J. DOE, refers to a *fiction,* and the *real* name, John James Doe, refers to *the real man.*

"The first man is of the earth, earthy: the second man is of the Lord from Heaven. And as we have born the image of the earthy, we shall also bear the image of the heavenly." — *1st Corinthians 15:47,49.*

"The last shall be first, and the first last ." — *Matthew 20:16.*

The Redemption of the soul includes protection from sin, and the purification of righteousness attributed to the shed blood (*sacrifice*) of Christ. (*I John 1:6,7*).

"He is the faithful witness, and the first begotten of the dead, and the prince of the kings of the earth who loved us . . . and hath made us kings and priests unto God." — *Rev. 1:5,6.*

Know Then Who You Are

One's ability to perceive — *one's awareness* — is directly proportional to the *level of one's ethics.* Humble though their station may be, these thoughtful ones observe what others do not; they look beyond the veil of tyranny that is human law and convey their discoveries to others, perceiving what no one had perceived before.

Laws today are called *codes* because they have been *encoded from their original form* so that the man on the street will be confused and not understand how to conduct himself and his affairs according to law.

Law is no longer *law* but a cornucopia of *code.* The Uniform Commercial Code (*the UCC*) is the achievement of an uncountable number of dedicated collaborators over thousands of years. The UCC is the culmination of a far-reaching, global PLAN to obtain absolute, legal, financial, social, political, and ecclesiastical dominion and control over the peoples of the world — through Commerce.

"And he causeth all, both small and great, rich and poor, free and bond, to receive a mark in their right hand, or in their foreheads: And that no man might buy and sell, save he that had the mark, or the name of the beast, or the number of his name." — Revelation 13:16,17.

Even so, there's *no mechanism* in the UCC that can ever bring about the *recapture of slaves* who manage to break free.

Redemption is deliverance from the power of an alien domination and the enjoyment of its resultant freedom. It includes the idea of being *restored* to the status of one who possesses a more fundamental right or interest. It is *salvation* from a state or circumstance that would impair or destroy the *value* of human existence or human existence itself.

The word *"redeemer"* and its related terms *"redeem"* and *"redemption"* appear in Scripture some 130 times. Although used to describe *divine activity,* these words arise in *human affairs* as well, and it is in this context that they must be first understood.

These words, as belonging to the domain of commercial law, refer to *the payment of an equivalent* for what is secured or released. The relation of the *agent* to the *object of redemption* is always — *in Scripture* — a person or another living thing. Its usage in *cultic activity* does not differ from that of a normal *commercial transaction.* In both cases a person or an animal is released *in return for money or an acceptable replacement.*

The Christ Idea displaces the notion of lack, limitation, want and woe, sin, sickness, and death.

A Cultural Obscurity

Incredibly — even though it permeates and dominates the lives and everyday activities of every man, woman, and child in America and virtually every living being on planet earth — and even though it's the most *senior form of law* in every country in the world — the UCC has been so brilliantly orchestrated by the legal masters of the world that it's become *a cultural obscurity* so well absorbed into society as to not even raise *an eyebrow of interest* upon its mention.

Even the general members of the Bar are for the most part ignorant of its far-reaching application and implication that dominates their lives as well. Most likely you never even heard of the UCC until it was herein brought to mind.

By studying the UCC it is possible for you to gain control of your life and better protect your family, your property, and yourself.

Know then who you are.

18
Come Out Of Her My People

"Come out of her, my people, that ye be not partakers of her sins, and that ye receive not of her plagues."
— *Revelation 18:4.*

THE PLANTATION called the United States (*not the united states of America*) has been operating on a war basis ever since *we-the-people* were declared to be its enemies by the 1933 Amendment to the Emergency War Powers Act that was passed when we entered the First World War in 1917.

In times of war there are *three parties* to the war. There are *allies,* there are *billigerents,* and there are *neutrals.* What *you* are depends upon your character and *status in life.*

If you are an *ally,* then you're one of the friendlies, but it has been proven in times of war that *allies carry indemnification papers* to prove their ally status. When Americans became an *"enemy"* of the United States on March 9, 1933, they converted their character from that of a *belligerent enemy* into that of a *friendly ally* by licensing themselves in the government of the United States by getting their *proper papers* that authorized them to be treated as *an ally in the war zone.*

However, if you are *a belligerent* and not *an ally* — under the *rules of engagement* of the international laws of war — anytime the military comes upon you — *a belligerent vessel* — the acts of war apply so they can seize your property, your crew, your vessel, and all persons on board.

And they don't need due process of law to do this. They can hold you in a military brig, *without due process of law,* until the end of the war.

They may go through the *illusion* of a trial or lock you up without any trial at all. The military doesn't need to get a warrant before seizing you and your things.

On the other hand, if you are *a neutral,* you can be stopped on the high seas for inspection but you can't be detained, — unless, that is, you perform some act of *belligerency.*

Yahweh told you to be not a lion but a lamb,. *Is a lamb belligerent? A lamb is neutral.* Why would you want to fight these government people anyway? If you fight them, *you're a belligerent.* It's no wonder your acts of war are likely to come against you. You ought to *convert yourself into a position of neutrality.* What should *you* care what these idiots do on their own plantation? — *shoot everybody on their own plantation?*

You are not a member of their plantation and you are not stealing anything off their plantation, so why would those guys be after *you?* Do you need their *war-power papers* to sail the high seas as a neutral? No. Not at all.

If we understand what *Yashua* (*Jesus*) and *Yahweh* (*God*) put into their Law Book, *why would we be at war against the world?*

What did *Yashua* say when he was before Pontius Pilate? He said, paraphrased:

"You are the one who claims that I am of this world. I didn't claim that. I didn't claim to be a king who would come against your corporate vassal states. What do I care what you and Satan do on your own plantation? I wish all of you clowns would get smart and come off

the plantation, but what have I got to do with you?" Understand, we're fighting a war that's part of *the idolatry that exists in our mind.* We're upset because we think those people are *our government,* and they're not doing what we think they should do, so we gotta take them down. *They're not our government.* They're a *military organization* that has no authority over us.

You don't understand *who they are* — or *who you are.* You fall for a bunch of presumptions and go to war against these guys, then you get upset when they treat you as a *belligerent* in their war.

When does *the law apply,* and when does *grace apply?*

The law is there for a teaching, The law applies as long as it's necessary to teach. For instance, if the law teaches, then, if you've done something wrong, when you come to see that you should admit it, you will repent of your ways, and make right those you have damaged. Then at that stage of the game, law and penalty end and grace abounds.

We get our *remedy through grace,* not *through the law.* We use the law to teach the truth so that whatever happens is what God expects from his people in life.

"Blessed are the [neutrals]: for they shall inherit the earth. Blessed are the peacemakers: for they shall be called the children of God." — *Matthew 5:5, 9.*

19

Public? Or Private!

THE CONCEPT of *public v. private* is by far the most important concept that you must master in the process of commercial *Redemption-in-Law.*

Black's Law Dictionary, 6th edition, describes *public* as: *"The whole body politic, or the aggregate of the citizens of a state, nation, or municipality. The inhabitants of a particular place; all the inhabitants of a particular place ; the people of the neighborhood,"* and *private* as: *"Affecting or belonging to private individuals, as distinct from the public generally; not official; not clothed with office."*

That which is public cannot be private since it is public — shared by all. Whereas, that which is private is not public and cannot remain private unless it is kept from the public.

Now, in which sector do you want to operate your life? It should be quite clear to everyone that operating *from the private sector* has some extreme advantages, — not the least of which is the total lack of *public regulation.*

However, coming from the *public sector* and having been educated in the *public school system,* doesn't aid this process. A paradigm shift is required *from the public to a private point of view,* to gain the skills necessary, especially in the use of words in your daily writing and speech. According to the Holy Scriptures, *your word is your bond (your contract).*

The *public sector* teaches us *public concepts* but nothing about *private concepts.* The words and phrases you most likely use come from the public side of the spectrum, since that was the way you were taught in the *public schools.* Your "heart" has always been with the *public side.* But most of these *public phrases and words* have *private counterparts,* and most are opposite in meaning.

For instance: public v. private; democracy v. republic; STATE OF NORTH CAROLINA v. North Carolina republic; NC v. North Carolina; persons v. men and women; voters v. electors; attorneys v. lawyers; color of law v. common law; agreement v. contract; legal v. lawful; revocable privileges v. unalienable rights; fiction/dishonor/injustice v. truth/honor/ justice; limited liability v. responsibility; insurance v. assurance; equity v. ownership; subjects v. sovereigns; slaves v. masters; employees v. employers; debtors v. creditors; poverty v. wealth; liabilities v. assets; equity v. debt; accommodated party v. accommodation party; offer v. acceptance; common stock v. preferred stock; taxpayer v. prepaid; subject to levy v. exempt from levy; negotiable (*transaction by fictions*) v. non-negotiable (*man to man*); paper money v. substance; police officers v. peace officers; negative v. positive; man's legal system v. natural (God's) law; the things of this world v. the things of God.

Always picture yourself and act as a man or woman from the *private side* on the *right.* Always conduct your business from the *private venue.* Using the words and phrases from the *right side* will keep you from traversing into the public domain. *Your words are your bond* (*contract*) and the words you use are the words by which you will be judged.

The *private side* emulates New Testament law — *the law of forgiveness and grace.* The *public side* emulates Old Testament law — the law of *execution of law.*

The Jews, in denying Christ and fulfilling the old law, practice *execution of law* as commanded by Moses. Anyone professing to be a Christian who embrace *execution of law* is not a *true Christian* since he denies the Redemption of Christ. We are in a period of *divine grace;* our debts have been paid by Christ. Only in the *private sector* will we find honor, justice and truth. The *public sector* is wrought with dishonor, injustice and fraud.

Acceptance, honor, and responsibility are our saving grace. Dishonor is death. *We operate under contract.* They operate *under color of law.* They carelessly revoke the public's privileges. We operate with our full unalienable rights.

Redemptors are the sovereigns, the owners, the preferred stockholders, the creditors, the employers and the masters — while the *uninformed public* remain the debtors. Any good accountant will tell you that *the assets belong on the right side of the ledger.*

Only a *real man or woman* can be an owner. It is physically impossible for a *fictional entity* to own anything. Only *a real man or woman* can be a creditor or accept value, it is impossible for *a fictional entity* to give "credit" to anything or anyone, since it has nothing to give.

Only *real men and women* can engage *in private (nonnegotiable)* contracts because only *real men and women* have the mind in which the "meeting of minds" can take place.

Only *real men and woman* have the capacity to accumulate wealth, assets, or equity and have names that are spelled *with proper English (cursive)* spelling. Along with *other public entities,* like corporations and public agencies, *the strawman* was created and designed to operate in the public sector, and all have been given names, as vessels, spelled in all capital letters. Government agencies, and other *corporate fictions,* have no eyes to see, nor ears to hear, nor do they have a brain of their own, and they don't have a heart with which to compassionately feel. They have no way of communicating with us except via *a transmitting utility — our strawman.*

20
American Bar Association Control

NEITHER LAW nor elected representatives govern America. Our nation is controlled and manipulated by a committee of lawyers, the American Bar Association, the infamous Bar who care not about us but about themselves and their wealth. In September 1995, for the first time in American history, *the inflow* of tax revenues was less than our government had to pay *on just the interest* it owes to the non-federal Federal Reserve on the national debt. In other words, our Federal government can't even pay *the interest* on the loans they've promised to pay to mostly foreign entities.

The crafty powers that control this great land behind the scenes are about to choke us into submission. The United States Corp. declared bankruptcy in 1933. President Franklin D. Roosevelt, *author of American Socialism,* declared bankruptcy in Executive Orders 6073, 6102, 6111, and 6260. At the same time, all gold and silver was taken away from *We-the-People* of America. This was done pursuant to the Trading with the Enemy Act of October 6, 1917 when our entire nation was placed under *an economic emergency.* This *"emergency"* has never been rescinded and we are still subject to the same *emergency declaration* today.

In order to bail out our insolvent federal government, the several incorporated States of the Union pledged the faith and credit of *We-the-People* to the National Government. This is how we ended up with the *Social Security Adminis-*

tration and the _Council of State Governors,_ among many other socialistic entities. On January 22, 1937, these organizations published their _Declaration of Interdependence_ in _The Book of States_ where they openly declared that all farmers (_land owners_) were no more than feudal tenants (_page 155, 1937 edition_). This was and is the method used _to literally steal_ private property from _We-the-People_ in order to _unconstitutionally_ benefit others without just compensation.

Today, a homeowner doesn't receive a _lawful deed or title_ to his land. Instead, he receives a _Warranty Deed_ whereby the State holds _the actual title and deed_ as collateral for the national government's debt (_the corporate body known as the United States located in Washington City_). _Nobody_ owns their land today; the United States owns it all. They only hold a piece of paper — a _Warranty Deed_ — that _warrants_ that an original deed does exist.

The same applies to motor vehicles. When you buy a car you are given a _Certificate of Title_ but the _actual title_ is held by the government as collateral for its national debt. You only hold a paper that _certifies_ that indeed a title does exist. In other words, even if you have no house mortgage or car loan, you still don't own them — the United States holds title to your property.

The previously mentioned _Council of State Governors_ is now the _National Conference Of Commissioners On Uniform State Laws._ This organization consists of only _Bar-licensed lawyers,_ the illegal and immoral monopoly that controls our Nation and our States. These licensed socialists — (_communists seize private land without just compensation_) — parade around with the unconstitutional _Royal Title of Nobility_: Esquire (_Esq._). According to the By-Laws of their organization, they lobby for, pass, order and execute statutory provisions to *"...help implement international treaties of the United States, or where world uniformity would be desirable"* — *1990-1991.* (*National Council of Commissioners On Uniform State Laws, page 2*).

In his book *The Tempting of America*, Robert Bork wrote on page 30: ***"We are governed not by law or elected representatives, but by an unelected, unrepresentative, unaccountable committee of lawyers applying no will but their own."*** And he should know; Robert Bork was a Federal Judge and Supreme Court nominee.

The *Bar licensed lawyers* have consistently done away with all *Constitutional and Common Law,* and have substituted an enforced *Statute Law or Codes (a.k.a. Law of Merchant, Uniform Commercial Code)* to keep *We-the-People* as *collateral* for a bankrupt United States. Is this freedom and liberty? Remember, the United States is *an artificial bankrupt corporate entity,* not *We-the-living-People* of America.

After World War II, *the United States, Inc.* once again declared *Bankruptcy and Reorganization* in 1950, — *Title 5 of the United States Codes Annotated (5 USCA).* The *Secretary of Treasury* was appointed as the *Receiver in Bankruptcy* according to *Reorganization Plan No. 26, 5 U.S.C.A. 903, Public Law 94-564.* Each year since 1863, the United States has continued to file *additional reorganization plans.*

On July 23, 1965, the *corporate United States government* blatantly violated our Constitution when President Lyndon B. Johnson signed the *Coinage Act of 1965* which completely removed our constitutional coinage and money. There was *no* constitutional Amendment to change our lawful money; Congress had *no constitutional authority* to remove silver and gold from our money. In fact, Congress was mandated by our Constitution in *Article I, Section 8 and Article I, Section 10* to maintain our silver and gold Coin (*U.S. Dollar*) under the equal weights and measures clause. We now have worthless paper *Federal Reserve Notes* (*Bills of Credit*) redeemable for neither silver nor gold. Whereas, according to our ordained *Constitution of 1787,* Congress has no authority to replace silver and gold coins. Only a *constitutional Amendment* can do so, and not one state has ratified such a change. Such an action is called *a de facto act* (*based on fact, not law*) and is unauthorized and unlawful, though *"legal."* The several States sanctioned and enforced this unlawful treason, *making it "legal."*

Since these *Bar lawyers* deemed themselves so successful in fooling *We-the-People,* they now feel they can do any prohibited act, such as *ban guns* that are protected by the Constitution (*Clinton and Reno were Bar members*). This is how dangerous and communistic these licensed *Bar members* are — trusting a *Bar member* is a mistake. The Congress (*made up of more than 75% Bar member lawyers*) passed the *Federal Tax Lien Act of 1966,* whereby the entire taxing and monetary system was placed under the *Uniform Commercial Code* (*Public Law 89-719*).

The UCC was written by none other than the *National Conference of Commissioners On Uniform State Laws,* the *Bar Lawyers.* When you hire a lawyer to represent you in court that *licensed Bar member* is *prohibited* from protecting your *constitutional* or *Christian Common Law Rights.* He has taken an oath as an *officer of the court* (*a military Martial Rule Officer*), and he is sworn to uphold the wishes of the State, *not yours.* No *Bar Lawyer* can represent *you,* he can only represent, *under oath and allegiance,* the corporate State government.

On March 28, 1970, Richard M. Nixon, *a Bar Attorney,* issued *Presidential Proclamation No. 3972,* declaring yet another *"emergency"* because the US postal employees went on strike. This is how the *common law US Post Office* was placed under the control of *the Department of Defense.* — *Dept. of the Army Field Manual, FM-41-10, 1969 Edition.*

Then on August 15, 1971, Nixon declared in *Proclamation No. 4074* that Federal Reserve Notes (*Bills of Credit*) could not be converted into gold. Once again, on September 21, 1973, a state of *economic emergency* was reiterated in *Executive Order No. 10033.* Then on October 28, 1977, *Public Law 95-147* was passed which declared that banking institutions are now under the direction and control of the *U.N.'s International Monetary Fund* (IMF). This Act *also* declared that the uniform value of coins and currencies of the United States shall not apply to obligations issued after that date. This is absolute proof that Federal Reserve Notes are worthless . . . Congress said so.

The United States is *insolvent* (*bankrupt*) thanks to the work of some very cunning lawyers. A permanent state of *"emergency"* exists in order to implement their *perversion of God's law. We-the-People* are obligated to foot the bill and have *unknowingly pledged* our private property as collateral, since 1863. The declared *economic emergency* has placed our monetary control under the *U.N.'s International Monetary Fund,* with the *Federal Reserve Corporation* as the depository, with the *Internal Revenue Corporation* collecting our "debts." There is no other word for this trickery and deceit but plain FRAUD.

"Woe unto you lawyers! for ye lade men with burdens grievous to be borne, and ye yourselves touch not the burdens with one of your fingers."— Luke 11:46.

Jesus warned us 2,000 years ago about the *Bar.* We should have listened. The Lawyers have stolen our nation, our freedom, our God ordained Rights, and our liberties; *and we didn't say a word.* These proclaimed *"emergencies"* have created over *470 Federal Law provisions* allowing the President extraordinary and *unconstitutional powers* through *Executive Orders* and *Presidential Proclamations and Directives* (PPD's). This explains why nearly every President has been a lawyer. Clinton had enough *emergency Executive power* to rule our nation as a *dictatorship* without concern for the Constitution or *Christian common law.*

Perverted *Roman Civil Laws* choked and ruined Rome — and America is following suit.

Under these *Executive Orders and PPD's,* the President may *1) seize property, 2) organize and control industrial production, 3) seize gold and silver, 4) send military forces to foreign soil, 5) institute martial law, 6) seize and control all communication and transportation means, 7) regulate and control all private business, and 8) restrict all travel, and even forcefully relocate people from place to place.*

The President can control the lives of every American in any manner he wishes. This is *emergency power dictatorship;* and Executive Orders have already been issued to implement all or any of these wishes at any time. Welcome to the real world of the Amerika in which we now live.

Senate Report 93-549 states:

"A majority of the people of the United States have lived all their lives under emergency rule. For 40 years, freedoms and governmental procedures guaranteed by the Constitution have, in varying degrees, been abridged by laws brought into force by states of national emergency".

We can directly thank the *Bar Lawyers* for this. *State and Federal Tribunals (our entire Court system is now made up of Military Tribunals)* have repeatedly stated that Constitutional and Christian Law arguments are *immaterial, frivolous, and contemptuous.* That's because the courts are no longer under Constitutional or Christian Common Law control. The Courts are under *emergency military control* where our Constitution has been thrown out under *emergency directives and laws.*

On January 17, 1980, the President and Senate confirmed another Constitution: *the Constitution of the United Nations Industrial Development Organization. — Senate Treaty Document No. 97-19, 97th Congress, 1st Session.*

According to Congress — *the supreme Bar committee of the United States* – our ordained *Constitution of 1787* no longer applies. The UN (*within its own Executive Orders and adopted measures*) has completely eliminated any rights of expression, communication, movement, assembly, petition, Habeas Corpus, and Religious Freedom because of *declared emergencies* worldwide. Under treaty law, the US falsely proclaims that it must adhere to these provisions.

Our lawyer created *de facto US Government* is controlled by *UN Regulations and Rules* — even though *"Fraud vitiates the most solemn contracts, documents and even judgments."* — *U.S. v. Throck-morton, 98 US 61, at 65.*

If we don't stop the "Bar" we will surely be placed into *communistic slavery* — *runaway representation* from high and lofty places.

"I know of no safe depository of the ultimate powers of society but the People, themselves. If we think of them as not enlightened enough to exercise their control with a wholesome discretion, the remedy is not to take it from them, but to inform them. When the People are well informed, they can be trusted with their own government." — *Thomas Jefferson.*

"Come out of Babylon, my people, that ye be not partakers of her sins, and that ye receive not of her plagues." — *Revelation 18:4.*

21
Esquires - And Who Really Won The War?

AS THE STORY GOES, there is a painting somewhere in the vast hallways of the Smithsonian Institute which shows British soldiers boarding a sailing ship, *muskets in hand.* The ship is in an American port, and the soldiers are returning home after the War of 1812.

There is a problem with this picture which may not be immediately apparent to the casual viewer. History books tell us that the Colonists won that war. They should also tell us that winners in a war usually take the guns away from the losing side. So why were the British soldiers boarding this warship, *guns in hand?*

The answer to that question was provided by a common law judge in the California Republic. He had recently presided over a jury trial in which *"titles of nobility"* were the issue. The jury was presented with evidence and arguments that *the original 13th amendment* that disappeared after 1812 did not ban slavery after the Civil War. The slavery amendment should really be *the 14th amendment.*

The *"real"* 13th amendment was ratified by three-fourths of the Union states before the War of 1812. It placed into the U.S. Constitution a specific ban against titles of nobility and defined a penalty for those who accepted such titles. That penalty was the loss of citizenship and the loss of eligibility for public office.

The common law judge, said that the jury had reached a unanimous verdict that the ban on titles of nobility had, indeed, been duly ratified as a lawful amendment to the Constitution for the United States of America. By banning titles of nobility and defining the penalty for them, the *original* 13th amendment was specifically intended to keep bar members out of public office throughout America.

The qualifications for serving in the White House, the Senate, and the House of Representatives — or any public office — all have one thing in common: the would-be office holder must be a "Citizen of the United States."

Since the 14th (15th?) amendment did not appear until 1868, the term "United States" in these provisions means the "States United," and "Citizen of the United States" meant "Citizen of one of the States United." In other words, Citizen of one of the several states of the Union.

The Constitution would have thus contained a specific prohibition against titles of nobility and a specific penalty for their use — the loss of citizenship and the restriction from holding public office. The loss of citizenship means that a Person who was born or naturalized a citizen would lose that status and thereby become an "alien" with respect to the united States of America. Since the qualifications for serving in federal elective office all require citizenship, an *"alien"* is disqualified from eligibility for these public offices (*President, Senator, and Representative, County Commissioner, etc.*), and a close scrutiny of the amendment's language did not reveal any provision for restoring one's citizenship after it was lost, for this reason.

The original 13th amendment does not contain any provisions for restoring citizenship by renouncing or rescinding a title of nobility. If the framers of that amendment had wanted citizenship to be restored to those who renounced their titles (*e.g. Esquire*), then the amendment would have contained language to make restoration possible. The absence of such language proved that it was not possible to restore one's citizenship after accepting a title of nobility. *The original 13th amendment* raised some very interesting questions of law. If a law school graduate should join the bar in the state of his domicile, he would join the elite company of "Esquires." In America this is the title commonly appended after the name of an attorney (*see Black's Law Dictionary, fifth edition*), and accordingly, one might say, "Once an Esquire always an Esquire."

If our up-and-coming Esquire should develop a successful practice, it could (*and often does*) happen that he might consider running for federal office, let's say the House of Representatives. Would he be eligible for that office, under the original 13th amendment?

NO, because the title of Esquire would make it impossible for that person ever to be eligible for public office. As a resident alien, that person would NOT be eligible for election to public office, nor would that person be eligible for naturalization. So, there would be no chance that such a person could ever hold such an office, under the supreme Law of the Land.

Let's take this argument one step further. Assume, for the moment, that John Q. Esquire gets elected to the House of Representatives, by some quirk of circumstances (*or intentional cover-up*). Would Mr. Esquire be a lawful occupant of that office? NO. Would Mr. Esquire be capable of exercising the powers and privileges of that office? NO. Would Mr. Esquire be qualified to vote on the matters which came before that august body? NO. If Mr. Esquire did attempt to cast a vote on any of the matters which came before the House of Representatives his vote would be null and void *ab initio* (*from the beginning*). In other words, his vote would not be a vote at all.

How many Esquires does it take to nullify an act of Congress? One? Two? Fifty-one percent? How many Esquires are presently seated in Congress? Is it greater than fifty-one percent? Is it greater than a quorum? Or does it really take only *one Esquire* to spoil the vote of the whole?

Maybe we should reconvene that California common law jury and put this question to them, because we now appear to have a really *big* problem on our hands.

If the Senate and House of Representatives ever consisted of members who were disqualified from serving there by reason of their titles of nobility, then every single act of those bodies would be null and void from the beginning.

A House or Senate consisting of disqualified Esquires for members would be an unauthorized assemblage of individuals, and ALL their legislation would be constitutionally null and void.

Now ask yourself this question: Since the War of 1812, the approximate time at which the original 13th amendment surely became law, how many sessions of the House or Senate were conducted by members who had *previously* accepted titles of nobility? If your answer is close to one hundred percent, then you are more than likely right.

The shocking fact is that every session of the House and Senate since 1812 has consisted of members who were attorneys with the title of Esquire conveniently appended to the end of their names. This means that every session of the House and Senate since 1812 has attempted to pass legislation which would have been null and void from their inception had the *original 13th amendment* not been destroyed.

How about the Trading with the Enemy Act of 1917?

There is a magnificent collection of research by a Dr. Eugene Schroder which shows how Congress amended this Act in 1933 in order to define *all Americans* as enemies of the United States government. Would these acts of Congress be valid if its members were Esquires at the time of its passage? NO.

How about the Federal Reserve Act of 1913? This Act of Congress created our Federal Reserve system and the debt-money-system to which we are all yoked, it would seem, for life. Would this have been a valid act of Congress if its members were Esquires at the time of its passage? NO.

How about the 16th amendment income tax proposal? This Act of Congress sent the 16th amendment out to the states for ratification in 1911. Research by Bill Benson and Red Beckman shows how the 48 states botched the ratification of that proposal. Would Congress have been authorized to issue that proposal if its members were Esquires at that time? NO.

How about the 17th amendment proposal? This Act of Congress sent the 17th amendment out to the states for ratification at the same time as the 16th amendment proposal. It purported to convert the election of U.S. Senators to a popular vote. Under the *"old" procedure,* Senators were elected by the state Legislatures (*resulting in much lower campaign costs*). Would Congress have been authorized to issue that proposal if its members were Esquires at that time? NO.

If the 17th amendment had never been properly ratified, then we surely have not had a lawfully convened U.S. Senate at least since 1917. Then all the treaties which were allegedly approved by the U.S. Senate since 1917 would be also null and void.

What about GATT? NAFTA? The Genocide Treaty? The United Nations? Round and round it goes — where it stops, nobody knows.

On the contrary, we stop in 1812, the year of *our second Revolutionary war with England.* We have not had a lawfully convened Congress at least since the year 1812 had the original 13th amendment not been lost or destroyed.

Now about those British soldiers who were boarding their warship, guns in hand, at the end of that war, in 1814. Were they the vanquished or the victors? Didn't they just finish burning the Library of Congress where evidence of the *original 13th amendment* had been kept under the watchful eyes of our government record custodians who fled for their lives?

What those soldiers didn't know was that the *original 13th amendment* had *"leaked out"* to other states whose record keepers did not suffer the loss of their libraries, where their *official versions* of the U.S. Constitution show a 13th amendment which bans titles of nobility.

Those versions do NOT show any ban against slavery, *which ban didn't pass until after the Civil War.* Something very strange has happened here.

During the trial of James and Sharon Patterson, the Judge of the United States District Court Texas-Eastern Division, when presented with a certain law, said, *"This is not a law that this court goes by. I take my orders from England."* — *Case 6:97-CR-51.*

Here, a *Federal Judge* confirmed the fact that *the United States is under British rule.* America has *never* been Free. *The Revolutionary war was a fraud perpetrated on the American people.* The *real purpose* of the Revolutionary War was to centralize power and make England's colonists easier to control.

All Federal Judges, Congressmen, U.S. Attorneys, State Judges, Legislators and most Attorneys know this, and are in fact British Agents. Their job is to keep the people in line as *productive colonialists,* for which they — the British Agents — are well paid.

(*The police do not know that they work for Great Britain; they too have been deceived, so we must not be critical of them*).

It is time that everyone in America know the truth. Let every Attorney, Judge, and Legislator know they have been unmasked, — *the United States is a British Colony, still.*

22
The War Of 1812

"Our Second War for Independence" — *The War of 1812.*

By their FIRST WAR with Great Britain in 1776 our forefathers asserted and maintained America's right to independent national existence. By their SECOND WAR with Great Britain in 1812 they obtained equal status for America in international affairs.

The War of 1812 was not based on a single cause; it was rather undertaken from mixed motives: *political, commercial, and patriotic.* It was not popular with many Americans. It was far from logical in some of its positions. It was perhaps precipitated by political party clamor. Despite all this, it established, once and for all, the position of the United States as an equal power among the national powers of the world. Above all — after the petty political and partisan aspects of the struggle are put aside — in this war the United States stood for a strong, sound, and universally beneficial principle — the rights of *neutral nations* in time of war.

It is now universally recognized, according to international law, that *"Free ships make free goods."* At the turn of the century it was good theory — supported, indeed, by good reasoning as well — but disregarded by the most powerful nations of the world. As a result of the firm stand taken by the United States at this time, these disputed principles were settled for all time to come.

The cause of the War that most strongly aroused the patriotic feelings of the people — though perhaps not in itself the main cause of the war — was, unquestionably, the *impressment* by Great Britain of sailors from American ships. No doubt, many English sailors did indeed desert from their naval vessels and take refuge in the easier service and better treatment of America's merchant ships. And Great Britain, at that time, was straining every nerve to strengthen her already powerful navy, so the press-gangs were constantly at work in sea-ports in England. Once on board a British man-of-war, the impressed sailor was subject to overwork, bad rations and the lash. (That British sailors fought as gallantly as they did under this regime will always remain a wonder.) But, it is certain that they deserted in considerable numbers, and they found in the rapidly-growing commercial prosperity of our sea-faring trade an inviting opportunity for paid employment.

As a result, Great Britain, with a large contempt for the weakness of the United States, *presumed,* rather than claimed, the right to stop our merchant vessels on the high seas to examine the crews and to claim as her own any British sailors among them. This was bad enough in itself, but the way in which the searches were carried out was even worse. Every form of *insolence and overbearing* was exhibited. The pretense of claiming British deserters covered what was sometimes *barefaced and outrageous* kidnaping of Americans, which just would not do.

The British officers went so far as to lay the burden of proof of nationality upon the sailor himself, and if he were *without papers* proving his identity, he was at once *assumed* to be a British subject. This insult to our flag was carried to such a great extent that our Government noted more than forty-five hundred cases of impressment from our ships between the years of 1803 and 1810. Furthermore, by 1812 when the war broke out, the number of American sailors serving against their will on British men-of-war vessels was estimated to be from six to fourteen thousand! In *some* cases American ships were obliged to return to home port in the middle of their voyage because their crews had been so diminished in number at sea by seizures made by British Officers that they were too short-handed to proceed. In no few cases these depredations led to bloodshed. *Were not the British intentionally trying to goad us into war?*

The greatest outrage of all — one which stirred the blood of Americans to the fighting point — was the capture of an American war vessel, the CHESAPEAKE, by the British man-of-war, the LEOPARD. The LEOPARD was by far the more powerful vessel, and the CHESAPEAKE was quite unprepared for action. Even so, her Commander *refused* to accede to a foreign demand that his crew be overhauled in search for British deserters. Thereupon, the LEOPARD poured broadside after broadside into her until her flag was struck, in surrender.

Three Americans were killed and eighteen wounded. Four were taken away as alleged deserters. Of these four, three were afterwards returned, while one proved to be an Englishman, who was then hanged. The whole sordid affair was contrary to the law of nations, and in itself, was ample grounds for war. Great Britain, however, *ungraceful and belatedly* apologized, and offered reparations.

This incident took place in 1806, six years before the actual declaration of war in 1812, but the outraged populous rankled all that time; and no event did more to fan the anti-British feeling in America, especially in the Democratic (*or, as it was often then called, Republican*) Party. Such deeds as this led Henry Clay to exclaim, *"Not content with seizing upon all our property that falls within her rapacious grasp, the personal rights of our countrymen — rights which forever are sacred — are trampled-on and violated by the unlawful impressment of our seamen. What are we to gain by war? what are we NOT to lose by peace? commerce; character; a nation's best treasure: — honor!"*

Meanwhile British expeditions of considerable size were directed against our seaports in the South. One of these brought General Ross and five thousand men — the pick of the Duke of Wellington's army — into Chesapeake Bay. Nothing was more to the discredit of the military strategy of our Administration than the fact that *at this time Washington, D.C. was left unprotected, even though in evident danger.* General Ross marched straight upon the Capital, seized the city, and burned it — and its archives — mostly to the ground.

The "sitting duck" was plucked, and the "original 13th Amendment" was lost.

Ross' conduct in the burning of Washington, D.C., was perhaps within the limits of legitimate warfare, but it has been condemned as *semi-barbarous* by many writers and historians. The achievement gave great joy to the English papers but was perhaps of less importance *geographically* than was supposed. Washington, at that time, was a straggling town of only eight thousand inhabitants. Its public buildings were not at all adequate to the demands of the future and an optimist might even consider the destruction of the old city as a public benefit, for it enabled Congress to adopt the plans which have since led to the making of perhaps the most beautiful city in America.

On the other hand, was it *really* of less importance than was supposed. In the process, *the original 13th Amendment to the Constitution for the United States disappeared among the ruins of the government buildings of the town!* The original 13th Amendment barred anyone with a title of nobility from citizenship in the United States. Had it not been for its disappearance, attorneys with the title of Esquire would not be able to hold positions in the government from that time on and forever more. This was the great achievement that gave great joy to the English papers.

All American *attorneys* (*Esquires*) are under allegiance to the British Crown — they have no rightful loyal place in the United States government, yet almost all of our representatives in the federal government are Esquires.

According to the "spin-doctors" of *The World Book Encyclopedia, Vol. 20:*

p. 26 — "The War of 1812 was in many ways the strangest war in United States history. It could well be named the War of Faulty Communication. Two days before the war was declared, the British Government had stated that it would *repeal* the laws which were the chief excuse for fighting. If there had been telegraphic communication with Europe, the war might well have been avoided. Speedy communication would also have prevented the greatest battle of the war, which was fought at New Orleans, fifteen days after the treaty of peace had been signed."

p. 27 — "A group of young men known as "War Hawks" dominated Congress during this period. Henry Clay of Kentucky and John C. Calhoun of South Carolina were the outstanding leaders of the group. Clay was then Speaker of the House of Representatives. Like Clay and Calhoun, most of the War Hawks came from western and southern states, where many of the people were in favor of going to war with Great Britain."

"The people of New England generally opposed going to war, because war with Great Britain would entirely wipe out the New England shipping trade which had already been heavily damaged. Many historians believe that a leading motive of the War Hawks was a desire for expansion. The people of the Northwest were meeting armed resistance in their attempt to take more land from the Indians, and the Indians had considerable British support. An American army was attacked by Indians at *the Battle of Tippecanoe* in the Wabash Valley in November, 1811, and British guns were found on the battlefield. The Westerners, therefore, were anxious to drive the British out of Canada. The South had also suffered a serious loss of markets. But the deciding motive for war seems to have been a strong desire for more land." (End of quote.)

There is no mention here about the *original 13th Amendment to the U.S. Constitution* that mysteriously "disappeared."

Because of Eli Whitney's invention of the Cotton Gin, the South was getting to be more prosperous than the North — and there was a danger that the banking powers in the East would see their monetary control diluted by the establishment of banking concerns in the South and the West. The moneyed powers-that-be could, perhaps, influence *attorneys,* but not necessarily *the common man.*

During the trial of James and Sharon Patterson — *Case 6:97-CR-51,* — William Wayne Justice, Judge of the United States District Court, Texas-Eastern Division, when presented with common law, stated: *"I take my orders from*

England. This is not a law that this court goes by." Herein a Federal Judge confirmed the fact that *the United States is under British rule.*

America has never been Free. The Revolutionary war was a fraud perpetrated on the American people. The Revolutionary war's purpose was to *centralize power* and make the people easier to control. All Federal Judges, Congressmen, U.S. Attorneys, State Judges, Legislators and most Attorneys know this and are in fact *British Agents.* Their job is to keep the people in line as productive slaves for which job they — *as British Agents* — are greatly compensated.

(Our police officers and military do not know that they work for Great Britain; they too have been deceived so we must not malign or attack them).

It is time for everyone in America to know the facts. Let us all work together in exposing the British Empire. Let every Attorney, Judge, and Legislator in your area know they have been unmasked. The United States is a British Colony!

Who *really* won those wars?

23
Treason By Design

Lysander Spooner (1808-1887) was a brilliant attorney from the *"country" of Massachusetts* who spoke out gallantly against *"The State."* Here are the final excerpts from the last chapter of his book, No Treason, for your legal and historical review.

***No Treason* excerpt,** by Lysander Spooner.

This programme having been fully arranged and systematized, they put their sword into the hands of the chief murderer of the war, General Grant, who had just become President, and charged him to carry their scheme into effect. And now, he, speaking as their organ, says:

"Let us have peace."

Submit quietly to all the robbery and slavery we have arranged for you, and you can have peace. But in case you resist, the same lenders of blood-money who furnished the means to subdue the South will furnish the means again to subdue you. These are the terms on which alone this government, or with few exceptions any other, ever gives "peace" to its people.

The whole affair, on the part of those who furnished the money, has been and now is, a deliberate scheme of robbery and murder; not merely to monopolize the markets of the South, but also to monopolize the currency, and thus control the industry and trade, and plunder and enslave the laborers, of both North and South. Congress and the president are today *the merest tools* for these purposes.

They are obliged to be, for they know that their own power

as rulers *so-called,* is at an end the moment their credit with the blood-money-loan-mongers fails. They are like a bankrupt in the hands of an extortioner. *They dare not say nay to any demand made upon them.* And to hide at once, *if possible,* both their servility and their crimes, they attempt to divert public attention, by crying out that they have *"abolished slavery!"* That they have *"saved the country!"* That they have *"preserved our glorious Union!"* and that in now paying the *"national debt,"* as they call it — <u>as if the people themselves, all of them who are to be taxed for its payment, had really and voluntarily joined in contracting it</u> — they are simply *"maintaining the national honor!"*

By *"maintaining the national honor,"* they mean simply that they themselves, open robbers and murderers, <u>assume to be the nation</u>, and will keep faith with those who lend them the money necessary to enable them to crush the great body of the people under their feet; and will faithfully appropriate, <u>from the proceeds of their future robberies and murders</u>, enough to pay all the principal and interest of their loans.

The pretense that the *"abolition of slavery"* was either a motive or justification for the war, is a fraud of the same character with that of *"maintaining the national honor."* Who, *but such usurpers, robbers, and murderers as they,* ever established slavery? Or what government, except one resting upon the sword, *like the one we now have,* was ever capable of maintaining slavery? And why did these men abolish slavery? Not from any *love of liberty* in general, nor as an act of justice to the black man himself, <u>but only "as a war measure," because they wanted his assistance and that of his friends, in carrying on the war they had undertaken for maintaining and intensifying that political, commercial, and</u>

industrial slavery, to which they have subjected the great body of the people, both white and black. And yet these imposters now cry out that they have abolished *the chattel slavery of the black man* although that was not the motive of the war — as if they thought they could thereby conceal, atone for or justify that other slavery which they were fighting to perpetuate and render more rigorous and inexorable than ever before.

There was no difference of *principle* but only of *degree* between the slavery they boast they have abolished and the slavery they were fighting to preserve; for all restraints upon men's natural liberty not necessary for the simple maintenance of justice, are of the nature of slavery, and differ from each other only in degree. If their object had *really* been to abolish slavery, or *maintain liberty or justice* generally, they had only to say: *"All, whether white or black, who want the protection of this government, shall have it; and all who do not want it, will be left in peace, so long as they leave us in peace."* Had they said this, slavery would necessarily have been abolished at once; the war would have been saved; and a thousand times nobler union than we have ever had would have been the result. It would have been a *voluntary union of free men;* such a union as will one day exist among all men, the world over, if the several nations, *so called,* shall ever get rid of the usurpers, robbers, and murderers, called governments, that now plunder, enslave, and destroy them.

Still another of the frauds of these men is, that they are now establishing and that the war was designed to establish, *"a government of consent."* The only idea they have manifested as to what *a government of consent is,* is this: *- it is one to which everybody must consent or be shot.*

This idea was the *dominant one* on which the war was carried on; and it is the *dominant one,* now that we have got what is called peace. Their pretenses that they have *"saved the country,"* and *"preserved our glorious Union,"* <u>are frauds like all the rest of their pretenses</u>. By them they mean *simply* that they have subjugated, and maintained their power over, an unwilling people. This they call *"saving the country";* as if an enslaved and subjugated people, or as if any people kept in subjection by the sword, *<u>as it is intended that all of us shall be hereafter,</u>* could be said to have any country. This, too, they call *"Preserving our Glorious Union";* as if there could be said to be *any Union,* glorious or inglorious, *that was not voluntary.* Or as if there could be said to be *any union* between masters and slaves; between those who conquer and those who are subjugated. All these cries of having *"abolished slavery,"* of having *"saved the country,"* of having *"preserved the union,"* of establishing *"a government of consent,"* and of *"maintaining the national honor,"* are all gross shameless transparent cheats — so transparent that they ought to deceive no one when uttered as justifications for the war or for the government that has succeeded the war, or for now compelling the people to pay the cost of the war or for compelling anybody to support a government that he does not want.

The lesson taught by all these facts is this: As long as mankind continue to pay <u>so-called "national debts,"</u> — that is, *so long as they are such dupes and cowards as to pay for being cheated, plundered, enslaved, and murdered —* so long will there be enough others to lend the money for those purposes, and with that money plenty of "tools," called soldiers, can be hired to keep them in subjection. But when they refuse any longer to pay for being thus cheated, plundered, enslaved and murdered, they will cease to have cheats, and usurpers, and robbers and murderers, and blood-money-loan-mongers for masters. **End of *No Treason* excerpt.**

Lysander Spooner established the Union's sentiments about *"a government of consent"* after the Civil War. One of *two encumbrances* that stem from section 2 of the 14th Amendment — Consent and Treason.

When Spooner referred to the *"debt"* he had written it as *"so-called national debt"*, and when he referred to *"country"* and *"peace"* he put these words in quotes. This is saying that such words were not his words, but the words of the ones saying such things. That should give the reader the impression that something was not quite right.

To set the premise of what follows, consider this segment from the Declaration of Independence:

"We hold these truths to be self-evident, that all men are created equal, that they are endowed by their Creator with certain unalienable Rights, that among these are Life, Liberty and the pursuit of Happiness. -- That to secure these rights, <u>Governments are instituted among Men, deriving their just powers from the consent of the governed.</u>"

Now look at this definition from the sixth edition of Black's Law Dictionary:

Citizens. Citizens are members of a political community who, in their associated capacity, have *established or submitted themselves to* the dominion of a government for the promotion of their general welfare and the protection of their individual as well as collective rights." — *U.S. v Cruik-shank, 92 US 542.*

Now, what government have *you* consented and submitted to?

The United States of America is not *your "country,"* according to international law! And the United States of America is not *your "nation,"* according to international law!

Furthermore: *it is a crime to vote!*

"According to *Bouvier's Law Dictionary, 1856,* it is a legal fact that all *states,* also referred to as *republics,* in the American union are *separate sovereignties, countries and nations.* — *Alexander Hamilton, Federalist Paper No.9.*

The first set of definitions that establish this are as follows:

Country. By country is meant the state of which one is a member.

Nations. Nations or states are independent bodies politic; societies of men united together for the purpose of promoting their mutual safety and advantage by the joint efforts of their combined strength.

In other words nation means a state; it is all an elaborate word game.

Lawful nationality, pursuant to international/constitutional law, is defined as: The state of a person in relation to the nation in which he was born. In other words, *your native state is your country ; your nationality can be changed.* (also see *US government Style Manual of 1984, chapter 5.23*).

A country is a state, and a nation is synonymous with state. All the republics of America together compromise the

"United States of America" (*i.e. the Union of nation/states*); the incorporated unit; the "State of the Union".

The United States of America is not your true nation. Your true nation is the State in which you were born. Unknown to most people in America, the main purpose of the 14th Amendment (to the Constitution) was to create *new citizens (U.S. citizens)* of an *alternate political system* — a new system of government that stealthily usurped the governments *of the original American republics.* Such governments are now *de facto governments.*

defacto: in fact. **de jure**: by right; rightfully complying with the law in all respects.

The 14th Amendment was instituted by Congress on June 13, 1866, and purportedly ratified July 9, 1868. Section 1 of the Amendment is as follows:

"All persons born or naturalized in the United States, and subject to the jurisdiction thereof, are citizens of the United States and of the State wherein they reside."

Most people in the *"Patriot Movement"* believe that the *"14th amendment"* does not effect them because they assume that they are not within the jurisdiction of the *"United States,"* since they live in a *"State,"* or they are not of African descent, so they believe it does not at all pertain to them. Sorry. *This is incorrect.* Everyone born within the jurisdiction of the United States of America is naturalized at birth or at "minimum age" by the 14th Amendment and is deemed a citizen of the United States under it — except Indians. (*but Indians can be if they want to*).

The 14th Amendment to the U.S. Constitution, section 1, provides, as stated above, that *"all persons born or naturalized in the United States, and subject to the jurisdiction thereof, are citizens of the United States, and of the State wherein they reside."*

In the case of *Elk v Wilkins, (1884) 112 U.S. 94,* the court stated the following in reference to Section 1 of the 14th Amendment:

"...this section contemplates <u>*two sources of citizenship*</u> *and two sources only:* <u>*birth*</u> *and* <u>*naturalization*</u>*. The persons declared to be citizens are 'All persons born or naturalized in the United States and subject to the jurisdiction thereof.' The evident meaning of these last words is, not merely subject in some respect or degree to the jurisdiction of the United States, but* <u>*completely subject to their political jurisdiction and owing them direct and immediate allegiance.*</u>*"*

Accordingly, a U.S. citizen owes allegiance to all the states. What's wrong with this picture? How can you have allegiance to every state in the Union if they are all separate countries or nations?

To further illustrate this legal quandary:

"The following shall be nationals and citizens of the United States at birth: (a) A person born in the United States, and subject to the jurisdiction thereof; (b) A person born in the United States to a member of an Indian, Eskimo, Aleutian, or other aboriginal tribe: Provided, that the granting of citizenship under this subsection shall not in any manner impair or otherwise affect the right of such person to tribal or other property." — from Title 8 US Code § 1401.

Note that it states: *"a person born in the United States, and subject to the jurisdiction thereof…shall be a national and citizen of the United States at birth."* Also, note that members of the several American Indian nations can also participate in the 14th Amendment's "political system," but such participation is not *assumed* as is to all others.

This is further defined by *Title 8 US Code § 1101(a)(22)* Definitions:

"The term national of the United States means a citizen of the United States." In other words: a citizen of the United States is a national of the United States.

So you still do not think that you are a United States national? Under the international rule of law a child takes on the nationality of his father. It is a fact that *only United States citizens and nationals can vote in elections.* Now, did your father vote? Do you really think that there are two political systems operating as one?

Pursuant to *presumptions — the legal operations of the 14th Amendment;* and *declarations by Congress —* you have one "nationality" (*one nation only*) — *The United States.* This *presumption* is repugnant to the original constitutional system.

Georgia and North Carolina are both nations by legal definition. Lets say one nation declared war on the other for some reason or other. If you were a member of the Nation of the North Carolina Republic — *which nation would you have allegiance to —* how can you go to war against Georgia which you also have allegiance to? You cannot fight on both sides! Simply put, *you can only have allegiance to one of the countries — your country — North Carolina.*

Pursuant to the above example — you may have heard that the Confederate soldiers in the Civil War were deemed

"Rebels". This is *a misnomer.* In other words, *brainwashing.* See this documented evidence from the books: *American Juris Prudence:*

Rebels. A term loosely but incorrectly applied to the Confederate Forces engaged in the Civil War. *(30 Am J Rev ed Insurr § 2).*

Why were they not Rebels? There was no *breach of allegiance* to their nations (*countries/state-governments*) nor did they commit treason against the Union to a foreign power! They engaged in *a lawful war* pursuant to the doctrines of international law. As a matter of law, it was not even a *Civil War* — it was a *National War.*

War. A contention by force; the art of paralysing the forces of an enemy. 2. It is either public or private. 3. Public war is either civil or national. Civil war is that which is waged between two parties, citizens, or members, of the same state or nation. National war is a contest between two or more independent nations carried on by authority of their respective governments. *(Bouvier's, 1856).*

Now, again, What government have *you* consented and submitted to?

Pursuant to the 14th Amendment, you have unwittingly submitted yourself to the political jurisdiction of *the federal government corporation and its private law.*

"The term *'national'* means a person owing permanent allegiance *to a state."* — *Title 8 of the US Code, section 1101(a)(21):*

This is the *lawful position* that one has under the law of nations and the original constitutional system as recognized by the Congress of the United States. *You have unwittingly breached your political allegiance to your native state.*

Here is the unconscionable set-up:

You have to be a citizen of the United States (*a U.S. citizen*) to vote. Check State statutes regarding voting regulations. The language is intentionally written to confuse people. If you decipher section 2 of the 14th amendment you will see that *the de facto states (governments) only represent people who are voters.* However. It is a crime to vote in elections: *"...the right to vote at any election... is denied... except for participation in rebellion, or other crime..."*

The replacement 13th Amendment to the Constitution: *"Neither slavery nor involuntary servitude, except as a punishment for crime whereof the party shall have been duly convicted, shall exist within the United States, or any place subject to their jurisdiction."* You vote — you consent to — you commit the crime!

You cannot create *"citizens of the United States"* without violating the inherent Constitutional premises that were established under the Law of Nations. Usurping the constitutional government[s] was done by having voters *unwittingly throw off* their political allegiance to their lawful state governments.

By voting as a *U.S. citizen and national of the United States* you join in the *rebellion* that is noted in section 2 of the 14th Amendment. When you vote, *you are in rebellion against your "rightful (de jure) state government,"* you give *tacit political allegiance* to the insurgent governmental system, *over and above your lawful state government.*

This *alternate governmental system* — which seated itself after the Civil War — is fully evidenced in section 3 of the 14th Amendment; this section, however, has been very craftily executed: The insurgent 14th Amendment governments have to uphold the original Constitution pursuant to other clauses in section 3 — this or the *de facto partici-pants* (*the government officers*) are considered to be in rebellion also.

Nothing was repealed in the original Constitution when the 14th amendment was installed (*but not lawfully ratified*). The Constitution is in full force and effect but being used in a different manner.

The *United States citizens* (*voters*) are the true Rebels in this Quiet War! And you are guilty by association by fail-ing to claim that *you are not a US citizen.*

This crime is treason.

Treason. This word imports a betraying, treachery, or breach of allegiance. The Constitution for the United States, Article 3, section 3, defines treason against the United States to consist only in levying war against them, or in ad-hering to their enemies, giving them aid or comfort. This offence is punished with death.

The treason clause in Article 3, section 3 of the organic Constitution does not apply. This clause only applies if one commits an act of treason when the Union is in a war with a nation foreign to the United States. Even then the clause in the federal constitution takes a "back seat" because the state of which one is a member has first rights executed of prosecution (meaning original jurisdiction). Hence, treason would come under a state constitution or under the prin-ciples of international law.

Rebellion. Rebellion signifies the forcible opposition and resistance to the laws and process lawfully issued (*e.g. original constitution of a state*). If the rebellion amounts to treason, it is punished by the laws of the *several/separate* United States with death. If it be a mere resistance of pro-cess, it is generally punished by imprisonment and fine.

Insurrection. A rebellion of citizens or subjects of a country against the government of the country.

Sedition, crimes of: The raising of commotions or disturbances in the state; sedition is a revolt against legitimate authority. The distinction between sedition and treason consists in this, that though its ultimate object is a violation of the public peace, yet it does not aim at open violence against the laws, or the subversion of the constitution.

Hence, treason is the subversion of a constitution, such as the alteration that was done of the state constitutions to make them conform to 14th Amendment mandates. The state governments under the 14th Amendment are not the same as they were, therefore participating is criminal.

To reiterate:

Treason imports a betraying, treachery, or breach of allegiance.

Insurrection is a rebellion of the citizens or subjects of a country against its government.

Voter registration is deemed *prima facie* evidence of treason. By participating you are agreeing to the system which makes one subject to the *international private law of Congress.* This is why voting is taught to be confidential. *Voters are actually criminal traitors to their countries.* Since voters have unwittingly tossed their constitutional state political governmental system aside, they are then treated as a *public enemy of the state* and given privileges as presumed traitors.

This whole scenario nullifies natural rights as secured by the original constitutional system. The common law of each State (nation) is basically discharged — the *de facto* States are then penal colonies operating under the Color of War.

So You ask, *"So what does this all really mean?"*

This is a legal scam to make you a true subject of the governments — both federal and state (*voluntary servitude to a slave, bondage, and feudal system*).

Welcome to Democracy!

Syllabus:

As you can see Lysander Spooner had great insight to the planned servitude of our American nations in his article *No Treason.* In *No Treason,* he also states that the feds instituted a *"secret ballot"* after the so-called "Civil War."

He said this (about General Grants "peace") in his book:

"Submit quietly to all the robbery and slavery we have arranged for you, and you can have peace."

The changing blow came after the Civil War.

The conversion of Americans' state citizenship or nationality, *under the Law of Nations,* was gradually implemented so as not to draw people's attention. People in the *"Patriot Movement"* have gone deep into the issue of state citizenship; but they have not found the true key.

The appropriate classification under international law is *nationality — not citizenship!* Technically, there is no citizenship: the 14th amendment system took it away.

As stated in *Elk v. Wilkins,* — a *"citizen of the United States"* owes political allegiance to the *"United States."* However, *inherent, constitutional political allegiance* is to your State, all other governments are *foreign* governments, including the federal United States government!

A true American is fundamentally an *alien* in reference to the United States Code as to its political system . . . and state citizenship in the premise of the organic Constitution created everyone to be an alien to any sister states in the Union as a matter of law.

The *"Pledge of Allegiance"* is propaganda planned to institute the *"One Out Of Many"* agenda — *"E Pluribus Unum"* — which is found on all the American currency.

This extensive scheme was contrived by words, agent provocateurs, disinformation, and planned ignorance.

Possibly 95 percent of the people in government do not even know this. Who does know? And are they willing to fix it? Until that happens: there is only one legally conferred method to remove the 14th Amendment noose from your neck.

This method, *Redemption-in-Law,* being congressionally granted, has been well hidden by design.

24

Democracy - *de facto* Or *de jur*

de facto: "not according to law, but in fact."
de jure: "according to law, by right."

THE DE FACTO GOVERNMENT cannot be charged with treason but the officials in the *de facto government* still must recognize the unalienable rights of the people under the *government de jure.* If the officials in the *de facto government deny the unalienable rights of the people,* the officials are in treason to the *government de jure.*

Even though the definition of a *de facto government* states that it is never in treason, the *de facto government* must still recognize the unalienable rights of the people under the *government de jure.*

But when you ask for your unalienable rights the officials of the *de facto courts* never give them to you. So is the *de facto government* involved in treason? No. Because *you have committed treason* to the *government de jure* so you are the criminal.

This true under *the laws of treason* in the Constitution. Under the laws of treason in the Constitution you're a criminal; and when someone helps those in treason *they' are in treason too.*

When the *de facto government* doesn't want to do anything in the name of the *de jure government,* but is compelled to — it *tests* you, to see what you're going to do. And since *they know that you're involved in treason,* the *de facto government* won't help you because if they helped you they'd be giving aid and comfort to the enemy and they'd become guilty of treason too.

So the *de facto government* sets you up with a *solicitation (an enticement)* to get you to *commit treason* to the *lawful government de jure.* Once they know that you have done that — even without your realizing it — *they're not going to be your friend.* They're going to be as belligerent as they can be because if they're *not belligerent* they're guilty of treason too. That's why *federal courts* treats you as belligerently as they can.

There's nothing wrong with the *de facto government.* The government is always right, there's something wrong with you. You don't understand what you're doing.

The government has *no duty* to keep you in line. You have a duty to keep the *government in line.* To do that you need to do what you need to do under the *government de jure.* If you keep your actions within the *de jure government* you are not in treason to it, and the *de facto government* must protect your right to do it to, otherwise *they* are in treason and when the *real government* comes back they'll all hang on the gallows, which they don't want to do. Understand?

We have to *remove the beam in our own eye* before we start accusing these people in the *de facto government* of having a *mote in their eye.*

"Agree with thine adversary quickly, whiles thou art in the way with him; lest at any time the adversary deliver thee to the judge, and the judge deliver thee to the officer, and thou be cast into prison." — *Matthew 5:25.*

Now what act of treason have we been committing?
Our major act of treason is voting!
The *military government* operates backward. *They want you to commit treason.* You vote for the officials of the *military occupation de facto government,* in treason to the *de jure government* that they have set aside but may one day restore.

Under *common law* the people have their own *private system of justice* of common law and crimes. They have their own *private laws and rights of privacy* into which the *de facto public government* cannot intrude. But when you volunteer to answer their *public questions* — *or argue with them* — you waive your rights *to private common law.* You traverse to the *public side* of law and commit treason to the *private side* — the *public officials* then give you what you deserve.

You say to that government, *"Logic tells me that you should do this for me."* If the de facto government did do what you ask they would be *aiding and abetting* someone engaged in treason, so they do what you do not want them to do. Sounds crazy but it makes sense.

This doesn't *seem logical* but that's they way it is — *get over it.* This way they can't be accused of aiding and abetting somebody engaged in treason, even if it is treasonous to their enemy. Since you're *engaged in treason,* what rights do you have anyway?

Can you see now how they have set you up?

It's not what you *think* it is. We aren't governed by what *we do and wish,* but by the Elite in the current *de facto military, militant system* of things.

Why does America seems to be falling behind?

It's quite simple. People aren't allowed to govern themselves. *Well, actually we are, but we don't know how. We've been brainwashed in the public schools.*

People are treated and trained like animals, *after all, aren't we derived from apes* and told exactly what to do by the Elite? Then the officials come and ask us, *"Why are you doing that? Can you prove that you have a right to do that?"* We are "guilty until we prove that we are innocent"; and we cannot. We say *"Let me alone, unless you have some kind of constitutional authority,* OK?"

The statutory system of law doesn't allow people to govern themselves by custom and usages. All such dictatorial law generally comes from federal government by decree. The federal government is not supposed to have any interaction with the states beyond the stipulations of Article I, Section 8 of the Constitution. Under Article I, Section 8 of the Constitution the federal government had a very limited ability to come into the states. They could come in and own property to build forts and arsenals, and stuff like that, but they had no authority to come in with federal guidelines for public schools, aid to education, or anything else not authorized under the Constitution.

However, if people *want to enter into commercial agreements* with the United States Corporation (*a "for-profit business"*) they're free to *voluntarily contract* to do whatever they wish to do. And that's just what we've done with *voluntary agreements and contracts.* We've established *treaties* between our nation-states and the *de facto federal government* in Washington, D.C. — The United States plantation.

The 14th Amendment formula tacitly provides subversive empowerment to the communist system presently in place, *the so-called democracy.* When a United States Citizen votes under section 2 of the 14th Amendment they engage *in the insurrection* of section 3 of said amendment hence *all voters create a rebellion against their constitutional state government de jure* which is deemed a crime under section 2; *such suffrage is treasonous.*

This passively brands them as *a slave* pursuant to the *insurgencies* of the 13th Amendment. Thus by voting *they voluntarily give away their freedom* that was protected by the *de jure Constitution* which is still in full force and effect by clauses in section 3, and this creates a *Quiet War* in which a voter is empowering the communistic totalitarian dictatorship of the United States.

In order for the *de facto government* to take over, the *de facto government* got you to rebel against your *de jure nation-state government* by participating in their's. You are then in violation of your *government de jure* and are subject to *their rule over you.* They must treat you as *an enemy* even of their own government or else they're in treason to the *real government de jure.* This is why the *de facto government courts* cannot and won't help you out.

So why do you vote for a government which by definition has to treat you as their enemy and slave? And you want them to give you a remedy anyway? What are you some kind of nut? And everybody says: *"Go vote and get a solution."* Hello?

If this deception starts growing on you and you begin to say, *"Who cares anyway,"* then you really *ARE sick.*

Few people participated in the federal government prior to 1933 but because the Elite made them so broke by the Depression of '29, *they were forced to go to the government for Aid.* Up to that time the farmers were doing OK and just wanted to be left alone. But when the banks melted down, *every thing changed from that time on.*

Consequently, voting involves one in the affairs of the *insurgent de facto government* and perpetuates the subversive Elitist's power wherein *"Governments are instituted among Men, deriving their just power from the consent* (in this case *"surrender"*) *of the governed."* This organic law is an American doctrine based on the Law of Nations.

Simply put: By voting you consent to *your enslavement* to the brainwashing orchestrated in the "public system" of government schools. One of the ten planks of the Communist Manifesto is "A Free Public School Education." Nothing is ever free but everyone *thinks it is.* Americans have purchased and are paying the prices for their *communistic servitude.*

The *principles of suffrage* as set forth in the Constitution had to be altered. What's suffrage? Voting. This *alteration* was made to destroy the republican principles inherent in the Constitution.

Constitutional suffrage is based upon land ownership. Land ownership is where the sovereign power of America lies. The Elite knew that "democracy" could be established and flourish with suffrage of the masses — *a mobocracy.* The mobocracy places the State in control of the people who seem to *want to be controlled.*

Get the picture?

The original Constitution said that suffrage was based on land ownership. OK? To go down and register to vote today you have to be in some way *attached to the land.* You have to be called a *"resident."* Right? So have they changed anything? You bet. *"Residents"* don't *own* their land; the land is owned by *the State, a la Karl Marx.* The

State removed all the voters *off the land* and put them on *commercial collective farms.*

None of the people are voting on the basis of having a title in the land. We're all members of a society that has *no title in the land.* We're all drifters. Therefore when you vote in an election today, you're not voting as a constitutional voter. You're voting as *some transient piece of property* attached to the Master's land, electing *the Master's local representatives* for His benefit not yours.

You're not eligible to be an elector anyway because *you have no interest in the land.* They took you *off of the land* so every one of you has no claim to the land. You're *itinerant laborers* moving at the will of your government boss. They call you *a voter, now,* instead of *an elector.* You're not considered to be the same people as you were before.

There is *no right* to vote. If you were an *elector* owning an interest in the land you would have *rights based on property rights.* Your just a *tenant* on the Master's farm and he has all the rights. He just wants to know *your opinion* that's all. Is your opinion important? Well he wants you to *think it is.* So he'll *let you vote by a computer* so his agents can fix the computer returns to suit his whims. As long as you are *participating,* what difference does it make *anyway?* You have no rights. So, how much input does a person with no rights have, to tell his Master what his Master can or cannot do?

Where did this *de facto government* come from? It's not established in any of our law documents. The people didn't bring it here. The people don't know *that it is here!*

So where did this *bastard, irregular, inferior, dubious, military government* come from?

"The kingdom of heaven is likened unto a man which sowed good seed in his field: But while men slept, his enemy came and sowed tares among the wheat, and went his way." — Matthew 13:25.

We sowed good seed in our field but while we slept our enemy came and *sowed tares among the wheat* and we are now doing things his way.

"Let both (the tares and the wheat) grow together until the harvest: and in the time of the harvest I (the Lord) will say to the reapers, Gather ye together first the tares, and bind them in bundles to burn them: but gather the wheat into my barn." — Matthew 13:30.

"Blessed are the peacemakers: for they shall be called the children of God." — Matthew 5:9.

So now go to it, and reap!

Epilogue
Do more than 50% of the people of America identify their government as the source of the nation's ills? Do more than 50% of the people believe that the government threatens their rights? Do more than 50% of the people foresee needing to *disobey the law* to protect themselves from the government?

Think about it . . .

Would you dare to remove the tag on the new pillow that you just bought? Would you dare to break the law and lead public prayer in a public school? Would you dare to drive without fastening your seatbelt? Would you dare to refuse to wear a United Nations Flag on your United States uniform as did Michael New? Would those two planes have reached the Twin Trade Towers in New York City *if everyone on those planes had been armed?*

What a paradox . . .

What does this tell you? That our *de facto government* has become American's own worst enemy. In a democratic republic, the government can't be the people's enemy. If it is, the people have no government at all. Understand? People give their allegiance to a government in exchange for its protection of their liberties, property, and their lives. If their *ostensible* (*de facto*) government becomes their enemy — which it has done since 1933 — by depriving them of protection — then a *real government* no longer exists. When, no one is being rightly governed, the people's allegiance to it dissolves.

In America, the government consists of actions by public officials consistent with the original 1789 Constitution for the United States of America. *The government de jure would threaten no one's rights.* Under *that government* no one would need to disobey it to protect his life, liberty, or property. *That government* Americans would respect — because *that government* would be *self government.*

But we don't have that kind of government anymore. Why not? Because of the politicians we do have today.

If Americans don't want politicians of that stripe, then why are such politicians elected again and again? And if those politicians *are the people's true choices,* then why do so many Americans distrust — even despise — their government? If the government is democratically elected, and yet the majority of citizens hate it and distrust it, do the people hate themselves?

Or is the government not the *self-government the Constitution promises,* but an *un-constitutional government of usurpation and tyranny?* Not the people's government but someone else's government? Someone else whom the politicians serve in preference to and against the people, someone else who contrives to elect these politicians again and again no matter what the people want, someone else who despises and hates the people? Only *someone who despises and hates the people* would deprive them of *self government.*

Who's that someone else? The Establishment, the power structure, the "hidden hand behind the throne" of politics — it goes by many names, but it's reality is always the same.

The existence of a power structure in a democratic society *isn't a conspiracy theory,* it's a *conspiracy fact.* When politicians and judges take an oath to support the Constitution, then turn around and pervert it, to advance their own power and the interests of their clients, that's *perjury.*

This is the situation in America today. The people can sometimes throw incumbent politicians out, only to discover that the new officeholders are marionettes of the same string pullers who made the old ones dance. No wonder more and more of our countrymen have concluded that elections are not the solution to their problems, and have stopped voting in frustration and cynicism. They've succumbed to apathy because they haven't yet realized that *a massive refusal to vote could retake control of the government* without the Establishment being able to do anything about it. Popular resistance to the *de facto government* would mean the Establishment's demise for many years.

Just think of it. *The common man versus the Establishment.* It's high melodrama. If only it could be made understandable to the average Joe. Most Americans already know that an Establishment exists and works against their interests, even if they can't identify its members or explain how it operates behind the scenes. We have to show them how to beat it.

Not by debating the fine points of political and economic theory with the Establishment's academic mouthpieces in conferences at the Washington think tanks. Nor by litigating test cases on arcane issues in the Establishment's courts. That's a war of windbags fought in circles at a snail's pace.

A radical Congress has to step in and in one stroke strip the Establishment of its principle power, — its ability to re-distribute wealth and regulate the economy under the Supreme Court's false constructions of the "General Welfare" and "Commerce" Clauses.

When *that* Congress acts, the people will support it.

25

The 14th Amendment Of Today

Most Americans do not realize that the organic Constitution of the federal government does not *cover citizens.* Its purpose is to govern world trade and to militarily protect the American republics.

Moreover, the organic Constitution does not *designed to confer rights* to Americans, it was designed to protect their *God given natural rights;* to guarantee *the common law* as the civil law. Such law is based on the customs and usages of a *society;* the society is not subordinate to the will of the state legislatures; the society is *self-governing through traditions;* no authoritarian law is used.

Under the organic Constitution of 1787, each one is considered to be a *national of his country; his state.* He owes political allegiance to *his country* (*his state*). He is subject to his state's laws.

Under the organic Constitution of 1787, the federal government had nothing to do with a *state nationa;* the federal laws did not apply to such people.

Nevertheless, all this has been changed.

After the Civil War, a *new system of government* was installed by the 14th Amendment. The governments under *this system* are referred to as *de facto governments.*

Below is the amendment which created *the new system of gvernment* that operates under private law:

Amendment XIV (*July 9, 1868*).

Section 1. All persons born or naturalized in the United States, and subject to the jurisdiction thereof, <u>are citizens of the United States and of the State wherein they reside</u>. No State shall make or enforce any law which shall abridge the privileges or immunities of citizens of the United States; nor shall any State deprive any person of life, liberty, or property, without due process of law; nor deny to any person within its jurisdiction the equal protection of the laws.

Section 2. Representatives shall be apportioned among the several States according to their respective numbers, counting the whole number of persons in each State, excluding Indians not taxed. [editor's note: all Indians are now subject to federal taxation]. But <u>when the right to vote at any election</u> for the choice of electors for President and Vice-President of the United States, Representatives in Congress, the Executive and Judicial officers of a State, or the members of the Legislature thereof, <u>is denied</u> to any of the male inhabitants of such State, being twenty-one years of age, and citizens of the United States, <u>or in any way abridged, except for participation in rebellion or other crime</u>, the basis of representation therein shall be reduced in the proportion which the number of such male citizens shall bear to the whole number of male citizens twenty-one years of age in such State.

Section 3. <u>No person shall be</u> a Senator or Representative in Congress, or elector of President and Vice-President, or hold any office, civil or military, under the United States, or under any State, <u>who, having previously taken an oath</u>, as a member of Congress, or as an officer of the United States, or as a member of any State legislature, or as an executive or judicial officer of any State, <u>to support the Con-</u>

stitution of the United States, shall have engaged in insurrection or rebellion against the same, or given aid or comfort to the enemies thereof. But Congress may by a vote of two-thirds of each House, remove such disability.

Section 4. The validity of the public debt of the United States, authorized by law, including debts incurred for payment of pensions and bounties for services in suppressing insurrection or rebellion, shall not be questioned. But neither the United States nor any State shall assume or pay any debt or obligation incurred in aid of insurrection or rebellion against the United States, or any claim for the loss or emancipation of any slave; but all such debts, obligations and claims shall be held illegal and void.

Section 5. The Congress shall have the power to enforce, by appropriate legislation, the provisions of this article.

End of Amendment XIV.

Under the organic Constitution of 1787 all *states* (also properly termed *American republics*) are separate sovereign nations and countries unto themselves.

Organic: real; original; in full uniformity with the 9th and 10th amendments.

Under the organic Constitution an American is a *national* of one of the *American states/republics/nations — separate "free" independent state/nations* as protected by the 10th amendment of the Constitution.

The United States of America formed under the 14th Amendment Constitution of 1868:

Under the legal effects of the 14th Amendment Constitution, one *"super nation/state"* is fictionally formed by the unified *United States of America,* in which the states are each deemed to be a *political subdivision* of the United States, or Washington DC — *federal areas, or states.*

The American states are *quasi-countries* of sorts, because Washington DC is acting as the *state or "national government"* of citizens of the United States — U.S. or federal citizens (*dual citizens*) — one *"federal nation"* created by the 14th Amendment to the *United States Constitution.*

Accomplishments of the 14th Amendment:

The 14th Amendment (*by operation of law*) takes Americans out of their native states at birth; where Americans are *presumed* to be citizens and nationals of the District of Columbia United States — *federal citizens.*

Moreover, the 14th Amendment installs a *new governmental system* under a *new constitution,* which *deceptively* runs concurrent with the organic Constitution of 1787. Americans are fictionally transported to Washington D.C. at birth, then fictionally transported back to the state in which they live in that *US political subdivision* (*country*) as a *"resident alien".* This *legal condition* further creates an unnatural citizenship, or nationality, turning natural born Americans into *"unnatural persons"* or *legal fictions.*

The Law of Nations:

Under the Law of Nations, based on principles of natural law, one is a *national* of the *"state"* in which he is born — his native *"country"* and nation. He owes allegiance to his *state/nation/country/government.*

Under the Law of Nations a *"national"* is not a *resident of his state/country,* he is simply a *national.* When one lives in a state in which he is not a *national member* he is a *"resident"* ,or an *alien, or a resident alien.* Accordingly he is an *"alien"* to every other *state/nation/country/government.*

Alien. Owing political allegiance to another country or government; foreign alien residents. An unnaturalized foreign resident of a country; also called noncitizen. — *(American Heritage Dictionary).*

Under the Law of Nations, the term *"human being"* means a man, women or child; but the term *"person"* is a national of a society, *or* nation. As a *national,* one is a *"subject" of the government* of such nation. Accordingly, any such *person* is bound *to the laws of his nation.*

Under the *Law of Nations,* the term *"nationality"* is the status of belonging to a particular nation by origin, birth, or naturalization (*origin = native*). A *"nation"* is a society of people bound in unity under a particular government by their *mutual consent.* The term *"naturalization"* is the legal process that changes one's *nation* (*or country*) from one *nation* (*or country*) to another — that grants nationality to *one of foreign birth.* Today, nationality has little to do with ethnic origin.

Under the Law of Nations, nationality can be changed, as a *natural right,* legally called *expatriation,* the changing of one's country and accordingly his nationality and citizenship. One's native country is referred to as his *natural domicile or domicile of origin;* and if one has *changed* his country, it is referred to as an *acquired domicile.* One's domicile makes one a permanent *"natural born inhabitant,"* or *"non-native inhabitant"* of a country.

Under the Law of Nations, *"citizenship"* refers to having political rights. One's political rights are protected under the Bill of Rights of the original Constitution of 1787. Generally, the term *"national"* and *"citizen"* go hand-in-hand.

Under the Law of Nations, the systematic and planned

extermination of an entire national, racial, political, or ethnic group is called *genocide* — a crime under international law.

The 14th Amendment Is A Political Cabal:

The *federal government of the United States* was getting little support during its short period of existence. There were few people voting prior to the Civil War. The 14th Amendment is the *instrument* that established support for the United States as an *alternate political system.*

The people would not have supported the Union over their nation/states, if it were not for the *force of the Civil War,* so they had to be tricked into supporting the United States cabal.

Governments are instituted by the consent of the governed:

A *"mobocracy"* had to be created for the United States to receive support. The support of the Union could not be obtained unless the people were taken over by the federal cabal, because the American states were sovereign autonomous states.

Unknown to most people, the 14th Amendment is the artifice and device that *deceived* them into surrendering their *national sovereignty.* Section 2 of the Amendment is where the *operation of law* is found that executes the *act of sedition against the sovereignty of the states.* This had all been sold as an act of rights and humanity. However, the main objective was to get enough *"bodies"* or *"persons"* to elect the officials, as justification for the newly established laws to have some legal force and effect.

Section 3 of the Amendment *installs the insurgent government[s]* and preserves the organic Constitution; section 2 of the Amendment *empowers it;* section 1 of the

Amendment *naturalizes all Americans* as nationals of the United States at birth; the legal language in section 1 actually creates a *dual-citizenship* on Americans. Such Americans are *United States citizens — federal citizens/U.S. persons* — and citizens of the state in which they reside. This in turn negates the natural rights of Americans' unalienable rights held under the Law of Nations.

A society is a *"nation"* under one government. A *"citizen/ national of the United States"* is a member person of that *federal nation* and is considered to be a *"United States person," or employee.*

How the 14th Amendment Works

Section 2 of the Amendment intices a *voting American* to tacitly throw off his *political allegiance to his rightful state government;* this causes his *breach of allegiance* to his government. This is *sedition, hence treason* — a betraying, treacherous, breach of allegiance.

His allegiance is then given to the *de facto governmental system* over his state or country's lawful government; he is then *politically bound to the federal government* and he is now a *"resident"* of the state (*res = object*) and is no longer a national of his country.

14th Amendment Citizenship

A United States citizen and national is considered to be a *resident alien* in every *"State"* (*country*) in which he chooses to live; he does not have the *natural rights* conferred by God that are protected by the original Constitution of 1787. He has *privileges* instead, granted by the federal and state governments at will, not by God; he is subject to both federal and state *de facto* statutes and laws.

Due to the legal contrivance induced by section 2 of the 14th Amendment, *all the states are in a war mode;* the civil law (*common law/custom and usage*) is suspended for participants, where all *U.S. citizens* are subordinate to the *de facto state legislatures* and are treated as *enemies of the republic in which they reside.* Such treatment is due to their *presumed breach of allegiance* to their lawful state governments under the law of nations.

The 14th Amendment creates a *cabal,* whose purpose is to pull all Americans into a *foreign jurisdiction* (*the federal zone*) to *impose upon them* what they are constitutionally protected from. The 14th Amendment makes *all Americans who condone and participate in this system* a "*resident*"; a "*thing,*" an "object of the State" — *of the federal and state governments.*

res. In civil Law. A thing; an object. In modern usage, the term is particularly applied to an object, to subject-matter, or *status* considered as the "*defendant in an action.*" — (*Blacks Law Dictionary, 4th Edition*).

The 14th Amendment scheme is three pronged: 1) It is a mechanism for government control; 2) It enables the federal government to implement an income tax for the world banking elite; 3) It allows both the *de facto* federal government and the *de facto* state governments to do business with Americans — *such as licensing; traffic fines; social security; etc., etc.*

Simply put: The 14th Amendment is a *subversive political cabal* usurping sovereignty of the American nations via the *ignorant consent of the people.* The Remedy To The Fourteenth Amendment is commercial *Redemption-in-Law.*

Epilogue:
Legal Fraud Caused By The 14th Amendment:
Legal fraud. Misrepresentation of a material fact made

willfully to deceive, and acted on by the opposite party to his damages. — *(Black's Law Dictionary, sixth edition).*

The 14th Amendment to the U.S. Constitution fundamentally negates the 9th Amendment Article in the Bill of Rights for Americans. This has been noted in cases such as *U.S. v Cruikshank.* Although the Justices in cases such as *Cruikshank* do not clearly come out and say it, it is understood that *the nations of the several American republics are in fact not politically autonomous as they once were.*

The fifty American nations still exist under the 14th Amendment, but this has been kept a secret from Americans. No *public notice has been given* to Americans that *citizenship in the corporate United States is voluntary,* nor that *the fifty American republics do not maintain lawful national governments,* as under the (*original*) federal Constitution of 1787. The scheme has been accomplished with *"NewSpeak"* — the clever manipulation and changing of words.

The scheme is commercially based— and termed *Statism: "the practice or doctrine of giving a centralized government control over economic planning and policy."* Statism is just another name for Communism.

Since the foregoing *legal scam* is fundamentally an act of *genocide,* government offidials have protected themselves, accordingly, by congressionally providing methods to absolve federal citizenship. You can use such *legal methods* to Emancipate yourself from the *feudal system the 14th Amendment created.* If you do not claim one of the fifty American republics as your country, and nation, you will continue to be oppressed by the *elitist nation* created by the cabal.

26
The Privy Token And You

You the man-child were delivered in birth and registered by an informant (*your mother*) for the purpose of securing the rights or privileges granted by law, on the condition of such registration *through her agent* (*the doctor*) with the Department of Vital Statistics.

The informant (*your mother*) confidentially disclosed material information of a law violation (*causa bendi; trading with the enemy*) to the doctor (*the resident agent*) that commerce by aliens needs to be brought under the control (*regulation*) of the government whereby a security instrument is created (*Live Birth Report*) that is hypothecated and made subject to a factor's (*principle agent's*) lien.

In effect this is a bill of lading or Manufacturers Certificate of Origin (MCO).

The Department of Vital statistics then issued a Certificate of Live Birth (*Birth Certificate*) or Birth Registration to your parents, but to your parents dismay, your name was changed to an all-capital letters name of a vessel in port. Why? Because of a Factor's Act (*causa debendi*). Factor's Acts are enactments designed to mitigate (*make less severe*) the hardships of the common law rule governing dealings with factors, especially with respect to pledges.

You are now a commissioned merchant requiring a FICA tracking number for accounting purposes as required by 15 USC §§ 1, et seq, but what you do not know is that you are now the surety of a dummy corporation (*strawman*) having an IMF and IRS account in Puerto Rico making you a foreign factor enemy, alien to the United States.

You were originally the principle to your all capital lettered strawman, the object of being government borne (*brought into existence via registration*), by fact of law, which is now the subject of the government that created you.

You are now your strawman's accommodation party, surety, and guarantor via your signature on the application for a FICA account (*your SS-5 application for a Social Security Number*) and as such you have become a joint *tort-feasor (joint venturer) for profit and gain* as well as have undertaken to insure the other *tort-feasors* for any loss or casualty during your venture on the commercial high seas.

What you don't realize is the fact that as an insurer, you have the right of indemnification — *to be compensated for any loss or casualty of your strawman's investments or advances as an insurer of the insured.*

Of course, the informant (*your mother*), without ever knowing it, offered her and her husband's biological property (*their goods: you*) to the United States Corporation (*your strawman's Principle*) as chattel, and the United States created chattel paper and a security interest in your strawman, and your strawman's Principle (*you the man*).

What you also don't realize is that during the period of *1913-1933,* such security devices were deliberately increased by cloak and design to accomplish the purposes espoused in UCC 9 §§ 204-208. You did not need to give your consent for under the common law theory of *"indebitatus assumpsit"* the informant's (*your mother's*) hypothecation of the biological issue (*you the man*) was all that was necessary to create an enforceable collateral undertaking to secure the creditors (*the United States Corporation and its creditors, the International Banking Cartel*).

Surely you knew or should have known that 12 USC § 411 38 Stat. 265, 63rd Congress, Session 2 allowed the United States Corporation to hold and receive such hypothecations and accordingly the ability to hold and receive such goods, chattel, and property as security for your strawman's creditors who made fiscal advances throughout your venture thus far requiring you, through your commissioned merchant strawman, to deliver up the hypothecated goods, chattels, and property by act of registration by a *fortiori cause debendi according to the Factor's Act.*

The social programmers bent on total control even set in motion a contrived Great Depression, a National Banking Emergency, Social Security Registration, and the like, to demonstrate the fact that they do not need your consent to do whatever they want to do with you. Assent is all that is necessary to create a valid, binding, and enforceable contract. But what you really missed out on is the Rule Against Perpetuities, but you, eager to go out into the commercial world to adventure and gain gain, never realized the ongoing operation of such a scheme. But one day an attorney advised you that *"you're blowing smoke in the wind if you think you're going to buck the system; they have the goods on you."*

Those "goods" the attorney mentioned are non other than the chattel paper that created the government's presumption of a security interest in your strawman, fully assignable to you through every conceivable *causa debendi* known to man.

There you have it in a nut shell. And it will most likely take you a lifetime to figure out why you and your strawman are subjects rather than objects of the government. You have no rights, no remedies, no standing in *judicio* (*War and*

Emergency Powers Doctrine), except to enjoy the venture, honor your agreements, *and keep quiet like a good little slave,* while the parasites attempt to suck you dry of your energy, your life, and your soul, into oblivion.

That is, until you come to your senses and realize that an overriding *superior security interest* (*Agreement/Contract*) is your only avenue of hope to rid yourself of such a cursed existence; actually a contrary agreement that is required by law and wholly enforceable by law. Their security interest in your strawman is your Achilles heel, your nightmare, your dilemma. And so, dear reader, when are you going to wake up and smell the coffee? When? When? When?

Your promise can be hypothecated as a chattel because it is personal to you, even though not yet in existence. You see, even though you were unconscious of your strawman's existence, your strawman is the *"privy token"* that forces you to part with your property.

Hidden Tyranny After 1910

The Chief advisor to President Woodrow Wilson, Colonel Edward Madell House, had this to say in a private meeting with Mr. Wilson in the early years of the twentieth century: (1914)

"Very soon every American will be required to register his biological property in a National system designed to keep track of the people that will operate under the ancient system of the pledge. By such a system we can compel people to submit to our agenda, which will effect our security as a chargeback for our fiat paper currency.

Every American will be forced to register or suffer being unable to work and earn a living. They will be our chattel, and we will hold the security interest over them forever, by operation of the law merchant under the scheme of secured transactions.

Americans, by unknowingly or willingly delivering bills of lading to us, will be rendered bankrupt and insolvent, forever to remain economic slaves through taxation, secured by their pledges. They will be stripped of their rights and given a commercial value designed to make us a profit and they will be none the wiser, for not one man in a million could ever figure out our plans, and if, by accident, one or two should figure it out, we have in our arsenal plausible deniability.

After all, this is the only logical way to fund government, by floating liens and debt to the registrants in the form of benefits and privileges. This will inevitably reap to us huge profits beyond our wildest expectations and leave every American a contributor to this fraud which we will call 'Social Insurance'.

Without realizing it, every American will insure us for any loss we may incur and in this manner, every American will unknowingly be our servant, however begrudgingly. The people will become helpless and without any hope for their redemption, and we will employ the high office of the President of our dummy corporation to foment this plot against America."

This comment was made 22 years before SS (Social Security) or FICA (Federal Insurance Corporation) was devised.

Did President John F. Kennedy attempt to reveal this to the American people at Columbia University in 1963; ten days before his assassination?

Is every politician anxious for his paycheck or for his life; should he admit the truth?

The Mark, The Name, The Number

NEARLY EVERYONE in the civilized world today has been assigned a number. Every nation that has a national debt is required by their multinational creditors to track the incomes of taxpayers. Treaties with multinational authorities require the U.S. government to issue social security numbers to its inhabitants.

During the Bible's end times it is said that no one would be able to buy or sell without one of the following three things — the mark, the name, or the number.

"And that no man might buy or sell, save he that had the mark, or the name of the beast, or the number of his name." — *Revelation 13:17.*

There are significant rewards for those who avoid the *mark-name-number* of Revelation 13:17. Those who resist the mark will be given *the harps of God* according to Revelation 15:2 and *avoid God's wrath* per Revelation 16:2 and *reign with Christ if they die refusing the mark,* according to Revelation 20:4.

There are significant penalties associated with accepting this mark. Those who receive the mark will be *"tormented with fire and brimstone in the presence of holy angels and in the presence of the Lamb"* according to Revelation 14:10.

Why then would anyone risk participating in this final *mark-name-number* system? There is only one reason revealed, to qualify for buying and selling in the marketplace. No other reason is given.

Shouldn't a number already authorizing your buying and selling be suspicious? Did you get a number so you could buy or sell? Did you get a number so you could buy or rent housing, or buy a license to travel on the King's roads? Did you get a number so you could sell your labor to provide for your family and yourself? Do you need a number to use as a government I.D.? Without a government I.D. you cannot cash a check.

The Uniform Commercial Code section 3-110 requires a government I.D. for anyone desiring to cash a check. Without a government I.D. your commerce is limited to the *crimes* of money laundering and evasion of the income tax. How can you be sure that you have avoided the *mark, name, or number* of the biblical beast?

What is the biblical beast? Daniel 7:23 equates Daniel's final beast with a final world kingdom, not a church, not a king, not a man, nor an Antichrist. The word Antichrist does not appear in the book of Revelation even today.

The United States is symbolized by an eagle. England by a lion. Russia by a bear. In Revelation 13 an entire con-federation of Daniel's beasts (*like unto a leopard-bear-lion with seven heads and ten horns*) has been assimi-lated by Daniel's fourth exceedingly dreadful iron beast (*Daniel 7:19*) that was to take away the domination of other beast powers (*Daniel 7:12*), consume and trample down the whole earth and *"break it in pieces"* (verse 23). This final beast kingdom lets the two horned second beast of Revelation 13:11 issue the dreaded mark of the beast. The two-horned second beast is the beast that causes all to re-ceive the *"mark of the beast"* of Revelation 13:16.

The first beast is often equated with the Roman Empire. This is consistent with Nebuchadnezzar's iron legged final world kingdom mentioned in Daniel 2:40. Do you have a mark issued by the authority of a final world power that is a confederation of beast powers?

After the American Revolutionary War, England's King George III signed the treaty that authorized the United States to exist. In this treaty the king explicitly retained his possessive title to the Holy Roman Empire — via the Vatican, — and to the United States.

The social security card has all the characteristics of the mark of the beast and there is nothing in Scripture that rules out a social security card as this apocalyptic mark.

Scripture — as well as our laws, regulations, and Supreme Court decisions, treaties, court rulings, statutes and regulations — show that throughout history those who forget God's authority are placed into captivity.

As will be shown, 1) our government has been surrendering to a multinational elite, and 2) we have waived all our rights by pledging allegiance as wards of our worldly *master/provider/savior,* the United States, and 3) a believer should not worship this worldly lord.

To make and end to the American Revolutionary War, King George III, in the Treaty of Paris of 1783, authorized the United States to exist, but he retained title over the United States of America as Arch-treasurer and Prince Elector of the Holy Roman Empire. The Holy Roman empire is explicitly mentioned in the treaty to be the treaty's authority that allows the United States to exist. Consistent with the beast powers of Scripture, the United States is part of the Holy Roman Empire.

Social security cards are issued by the Secretary of the Treasury of the United States but the Secretary of the Treasury is not an officer of the United States government. He is the Arch-treasurer of the Holy Roman Empire just as the treaty says. Many have tried to obtain a copy of his oath of office but no oath seems to exist.

The United States went bankrupt as of March 4, 1933. Five days later, on the 9th, domestic transactions were no longer excluded from the Trading With The Enemy Act of 1917 (*40 Stat L. 411, § 5(b)*) so Trading with the Enemy is now illegal unless authorized by license of the government.

We are the enemy of the occupation forces of Rome. Trading with the enemy has always been illegal but now *our domestic trade* is considered to be with an enemy foreign to our de facto government, and that enemy are us.

Domestic transactions can now be regulated and infractions thereof punished. Domestic transactions are illegal unless authorized by a license having a number, otherwise no man might buy or sell. It is illegal to buy and sell in America unless your transactions are with persons who have surrendered to that foreign estate, the United States.

The multinational elite is already pre-authorized by Congress to control your buying and selling with **"actions, regulations, rules, licenses, orders, and proclamations heretofore or hereafter taken."** It is the very same multinational authority that issues our social security cards.

Title 12 of the United States Code § 95(b) gives the Secretary of the Treasury complete power over us. Whatever actions he wants to take to control our lives are already *pre-authorized by law.* His actions *"heretofore or hereafter taken"* have already been *pre-approved* by Congress since 1933. (*This all fits in with Revelation 13:10, if anyone "shall go into captivity"*).

The Social Security Act has no provision for a trust fund or insurance. In fact, it would be unconstitutional if it did have a trust fund. (*David v. Boston, 89 F2d 368*). Even the supreme Court says that there is never a contractual obligation for the government to have to pay social security benefits because no one has a contractual right to any benefits at all. (*Fleming v. Nestor, 363 US 603*). In fact it is the official U.S. government public policy that only federal welfare applicants are required to have a social security number (SSN).

Social security numbers are only for federal welfare applicants. No law has ever required a worker to get a social security number. Neither has a court ever required a worker to get a social security number. According to Title 26 Code of Federal Regulations § 31.3402(p) *"furnishing Form W-4 shall constitute a request for withholding."* U.S. Citizens were not subject to withholding according to the recently repealed Title 26 Code of Federal Regulations § 1.1441-5 entitled *"Claiming to be a person not subject to withholding."*

Even the Social Security Administration admits that it is unaware of any law or regulation requiring the social security number to be used for employment purposes.

It is highly unlikely that you *ever* qualified for a social security number anyway. Social Security Act § 205(c)(2)(B)(i) allows social security cards to be issued to those who need government funds. The application for a social security card is an application to become a ward of the state. You signed a financing statement whereby they agreed to finance your benefits in exchange for something else. This can be upheld in any court.

Once you voluntarily asked to be a ward of your master, the state, you are chained to their chain of command. While you are in their house, on their plantation, you must obey their rules, no matter how abhorrent or repugnant the rules become. The Supreme Court in the *Ashwander* case said that **anyone who takes federal benefits cannot challenge their rules.** Caesar has become Lord. You cannot obey more than one Lord.

By asking to be a ward of the state, you have created a host of providers to regulate you, judge you, and save you, as your Savior. This is the moral equivalent of having other lords before god in violation of the First Commandment of God's Law.

By applying for a social security card you applied for federal benefits. Christians should not associate with freeloaders according to 2 Thesalonians 3:6-14. Therefore a Christian does not qualify for a social security number. But, of course, we all have a social security number, don't we. In this respect all of us have sinned and fall short of the glory of God. **Thank heaven God forgives sin.**

The *"enumeration at birth"* program was entirely voluntary until November of 1996 when children were for the first time issued numbers at birth regardless of parental objections. Congress claims that the GATT treaty (*GATT means General Agreement on Tariffs and Trade*) requires all newborn babies in America to receive a social security card, although the Social Security Administration says this is not so.

The GATT treaty is closely associated with a world power that sits upon many waters and has boldly vanquished, conquered, and subdued all Americans and put them into involuntary servitude to them.

A Christian name is a proper noun and has the first letter capitalized, with the remainder of each name in lower case. A proper noun is never spelled with all capitalized letters.

Your can no longer get a government I.D. with a Christian name. No one can get a government I.D. with a proper noun Christian name.

According to Article VI of the United States Constitution, treaties are now considered to be equal to the Constitution as the supreme law of the land. A 1797 treaty correctly states, *"the government of the United States is not in any sense founded on the Christian Religion."*

Applying for a social security number waives your right to earn wages on a *quid pro quo* (*substance for substance*) basis. This is what makes your wages taxable under § 801 of the Social Security Act. If you had a legal right to earn wages, the government would protect your right against taxable wages. You cannot agree to eat at the public trough without agreeing to the strings attached. Since your labor can now be taxed at any rate they want to take, they use your *future wages* for collateral on the national debt.

Anyone who has a social security number has changed his citizenship from the *country/state* of his birth to a Catholic owned feudal estate (*according to the word "cession" in the U.S. Constitution*) and has been seized by a multinational financial network as collateral for its debt.

The Supreme Court said, *"The citizen cannot complain because he has voluntarily submitted himself to such a form of government."* — *(92 US 551).*

Social Security is pure orthodox socialism. Socialists can not believe in the Scriptures. Socialists can't become citizens. Never could, still can't. — *(81 Fed 358).*

U.S. government regulations for assigning social security numbers to newborn children have been established by the United Nations headquarters district of New York.

You gave up your right to vote in a republic, your gave up

your right to a trial by jury, and you will soon get a national I.D. card. The law is already in place.

Most Americans have been systematically deceived bit by bit, *"precept upon precept, line upon line, line upon line, here a little, there a little,"* so that they might be ensnared into accepting a counterfeit government. Through small incremental compromises, America has been transformed from a holy nation into a nation that will receive the due penalty for its sins.

All the circumstances involving the mark are circumstances created in small incremental steps by socialists who are deceived and love not the truth. Throughout history, God has allowed pagans to take into captivity any nation that obeys a counterfeit authority. The conquering nations are instruments of His discipline.

The term "worship" can include swearing a perjury oath on an application form. Your signature is a type of worship. An oath is a religious ceremony.

Can you take the mark of the beast without your consent? Yes.

Those who have received the mark have been deceived. It takes wisdom to understand the number of the beast. (*Revelation 13:18*). A name or a number or a mark authorizes buying and selling. (*verse 17*). It takes wisdom to understand the beast's identity. (*Rev. 17:9*). 2 Thesalonians 2:3 speaks of deceivableness and delusion in the end times. The two horned second beast *"deceiveth them that dwell on the earth"* to cause them to worship the first beast. (*Rev. 13:14*). A false prophet will influence the kings of the earth. Men will turn to cleverly devised fables. And you will unknowing take the mark of the beast that will authorize you to buy and sell.

When you applied for permission to buy and sell you created a host of saviors to regulate your life. These man-made idols demand worship, provide, protection, and attempt to insure you against all harm.

But there is remedy. There is hope

Nowhere are we told that a *repentant* worshiper of the beast will be doomed. Only the unpardonable sin will be doomed. (*Matt. 12:31 and Mark 3:29*). Contracts signed under deception are *ab initio* (*from the beginning*) voidable.

Throughout history a brave few Christians have refused to honor Caesar as their lord. They were fed to the lions. When Emperor Decius issued an edict commanding sacrifice to their gods, those who wanted to live were allowed to burn a bit of incense. They were then issued a *certificate of compliance.* They complied with federal law.

But those who refused to acknowledge this lordship went to their deaths. They were told to obey their government . . . that their government is ordained by god . . . that they would be *martyrs without a cause* if they persisted in their strange beliefs.

You too were asked to burn a little incense. You were asked to sign an oath under penalty of perjury to your new lord. When you signed the oath you received a certificate that allows you to buy and sell. With your oath you worship a mighty provider in the place of your Lord.

Satan told Jesus that he (*Satan*) had power over *"all the kingdoms of the world"* and that he could give it to whomsoever he would. (*Luke 4:5-6*).

But the Lord rebutted and disputed this lie.

HARDCORE REDEMPTION-IN-LAW

29

The Endtime Beast

"And the serpent cast out of his mouth water as a flood after the woman and went to make war with her. . . to devour her" — *Revelation 12:15-17 and 12:4.*

THE ENDTIME BEAST is a system of law borrowed from the law of the sea implemented inland so that the *"ecclesia"* (*the remnant*) are forced into earnest demonstration.

This system of law is patterned after the maritime trust that transfers the commercial interests of the people, called "suretyship," to alien strangers wherein commerce knows no bounds and is typified by a flood.

The woman is non other than the *real true bona fide seed* of Abraham, Isaac, and Jacob — their progeny of today.

This "casting out" occurred in the early 1900's when the United States of America implemented a new system of registration which operates to implement a "factor's lien," a warehouseman's lien, over the registered goods and chattel paper covering the "vessel" that is defined as a "citizen of the United States." (*Title 46 USC*).

Under the Trading with the Enemy Act and the War Powers Act of October 6, 1917, citizens of the United States are considered to be "alien enemies" of the United States and are required to be either *registered or licensed* so that *inland piracy* can ensue as a system of commerce and trade.

This *inland piracy* is so *avaricious* (*greedy for gain*) as to leave the unknowing, the unbelieving, the ignorant, and the indifferent lost in disarray — deluded and totally unaware of their predicament.

The key to prevailing in such a war, is to have perfected an overriding superior interest, or *security interest,* in the goods, cargo, and *registration-chattel-paper* of the vessel — the strawman, dummy corporation, *ens legis,* all upper-case-fiction, *nom de guerre, nom de plume, idem sonaris,* mirror image of the *real* flesh-and-blood woman or man.

The Redemption-in-Law process — *an awakening revelation spiritual regeneration* — reveals that the perpetrators of this Beast system have a *legal commitment* to guarantee the obligations of your strawman.

30
The Matrix

matrix. "*something within which something else originates or develops; an* impression *used for mass-producing duplicates of the original.*" — *Webster's Dictionary.*
"Judge not according to the appearance, but judge righteous judgment." — *John 7:24.*

When our mortal senses tell us that railroad tracks come together in the distance we know that the tracks don't come together. Our judgment is not according to how the rails appear as reality to our senses. We judge by other criteria.

The movie *The Matrix* has moments that relate to the teachings of Jesus regarding unreality and reality. Discounting some violence and bad language, *The Matrix* has become a hint for people not to completely trust the five senses to always report a totally accurate version of reality.

There are innovations in computers today that virtually imitate the sounds and visual information of the real world in the three dimensions of height, width and depth. In computer generated virtual reality a familiar human scene is not only projected in front of a person's senses, a person finds himself in the middle of the scene walking around and touching things. The computer generated scene is called "virtual reality." The term virtual reality means not an *actual* reality.

The word virtual means, *in effect but not in fact.* In analogy, 2 x 2 = 5 may be *very close to the truth,* but it isn't the truth, it's an error, not a fact. Even though the 5 is only one digit away from the 4, that doesn't make the error the truth, although it *seems* to.

Computer experts plan to create more and more sophisticated scenes of generated reality and gradually connect them together into a collective virtual reality. Furthermore, three avenues of human memory, the past, the present, and the future, are also being configured into scenes of virtual reality. This version of human reality could mean, for example, that a person could be led to believe he had been on a vacation to a Caribbean island without leaving town! A person could be convinced he is there in some virtual place when *in reality he is not there.*

That *our whole human experience* might be generated as a virtual reality by an ominous outside force is a mind-boggling concept. That's what the movie *The Matrix* proposes. A movie like *The Matrix* could provoke a lot of discussion about *real reality* and *virtual reality.*

When we dream we often believe we are there in our dream. When events we are dreaming don't seem logical to us we are not usually bothered by the illogical things going on. But our view of the *realness* of a dream changes when we see the reality of our conscious world as we begin to wake up. What was believed real before, becomes unreal, as we come out of the dream.

"Come out from among them, and be separate, saith the Lord . . ." *— 2 Cor. 6:17.*

In *The Matrix* a few people become inspired enough to escape the dream and find reality.

These few people learn that their mortal existence is being generated by a computer program foisted on the five senses. They decide not to be self-deceived any longer. They explore the truth of reality beyond the senses. They begin to understand that mortal existence is a state of self-deception and not the truth of being.

The Bible teaches that *"The earth is the Lord's and the fullness thereof."* — *Psalm 24:1.* The collective mind of mortals could be therefore thought of as a *"mortal mind."* Mortal mind would have us *not perceive correctly* this truth that the earth belongs to the Lord. The Lord is Spirit, the Creator, or divine Mind. But *mortal mind* — the collective mind of mortals — would project its *supposed* reality on human beings claiming that we are strictly *physical beings* who are trapped in matter and cycles of time. The *matrix of spiritual reality* is obscured by the secondary, collective pictures projected by mortal mind on us as humans.

When our spiritual perception of reality becomes attuned to Spirit as the Creator of *real,* not *virtual* reality, we begin to perceive that there is something not quite right or complete with the picture of *material reality* that is foisted on our senses by mortal mind. We sense that there is *more to life* than we can ever picture or describe.

Could it be that the five senses, and the information projected by mortal mind to our five senses, is a simulated *"secondary version"* of reality? Mortal mind's projection of mortal life is not the *primary spiritual life* created by God. Could mortal existence simply be a *vast virtual reality* foisted on us by mortal mind? This virtual reality presents the *illusion of spiritual truth,* so we must avoid being deceived by mortal appearances.

"Judge not according to the appearance, but judge righteous judgement." — *John 7:24.*

In Jesus' analogy of the tares and the wheat, perhaps the reason Jesus told us *not* to separate the tares from wheat *until we could tell the difference, one from another,* is because in the mingling of truth and error they appear so alike. Even though $2 \times 2 = 5$ includes the truth that $2 \times 2 = 4$, a *reality seeker* has to avoid being deceived by appearances and similarities. ***"The proof of the pudding is in the pie."*** The *truth* is discovered in demonstration.

God's Blueprint Is The Primary Reality

God, *the divine Mind,* is the generator of spiritual reality. Mortal mind tries to be a *second god* but all it can do is mimic what is already created by God. In the process of mimicking God, mortal mind *perverts its views* of spiritual reality with *material concepts* by inducing scores of deceptions and false beliefs. We err when we suppose mortality to be the *matrix of immortality.* When we believe this to be true, we are being convinced of *virtual reality,* not the basic *spiritual reality* created by God.

At least one person has seen this original, primary, *spiritual reality.* He is Jesus the Christ, our Saviour from the *virtual reality* called *"the world."*

"Jesus beheld in Science the perfect man, who appeared to him where sinning mortal man appears to mortals. In this perfect man the Savior saw God's own likeness, and this correct view of man healed the sick." (S&H 476: 32).

When we entertain the *correct view* of God's reality we supercede *virtual reality* and see the truth. The *correct view of reality* proves the underlying *reality* to be spiritual and good.

"And God saw every thing that he had made, and, behold, it was very good." — *Genesis 1:31.*

Some people say that a divine healing is waking up from a dream.

How so? Inspired thoughts and prayers occasionally break through mortal mind's *deceptive, projected, virtual reality.* The result is improved ideas. Healing changes the illusive material world. It's like *waking up* more and more each day. When the blueprint of the *primary reality* presents itself, it shines through the *virtual reality* and orchestrates corrections. *These spiritual glimpses of prime reality color mortal mind's reality, spawning the divine ideas where corrective healing takes place.*

Our Task

It's not easy to keep the original basic *spiritual reality* before one's conscious thought, but that is the *ever present task* of a Christian. Jesus recommended to *all his followers* to go into the closet of inward stillness and shut the door, and pray. Could Jesus not mean, concerning the closet door, to shut it closed on the view of reality that is not God's?

One reason our prayers may be ineffective is because we are tempted, and convinced by *appearances* that reality is *material* and *NOT spiritual.* Material concepts of life subtly creep into our sense of awareness, *and we become numb,* we become trapped in our false belief that the *material view* is all there is to existence. *The material view of reality* bombards our prayers with false beliefs, instead of *the basic truths of spiritual existence.*

Jesus said, **"God is Spirit: and they that worship him must worship him in spirit and in truth."** — *John 4:24.*

This means *to NOT worship* through material reality. The thoughts of reality that we accept determine whether or not our thoughts are material or spiritual when we pray. If our words and thoughts are not related to *spiritual reality,* then

— as Shakespeare well discerned — *"Words without thoughts, never to heaven go."*

The following analogy separates the *material version* of reality from the *spiritual version* of reality.

When we go outside, we look down and see the flat surface of ground we're standing on. Actually we're standing at the center of a circle. The ground we're standing on is at the center of the circle we call the earth. *One version of reality* says we're standing on a *flat surface.* A larger view of reality says we're standing on *the surface of a sphere.*

The *flat surface* represents the *finite,* that has both a beginning and an end; whereas the *sphere* represents the *infinite,* without beginning or end. The *flat surface* represents *illusion,* the belief in a self-made, temporary, material existence, whereas the *sphere* represents *good,* the self-existent, and eternal individuality of our Creator, God.

Even though they *seem to touch,* one is still a straight line having a beginning and an end, and the other is a never ending curve. Even though there *seems to be two versions of reality,* one is *material* and the other is *spiritual. One is illusive and the other is real.*

The American Indians caught glimpses of the underlying reality of life, when the called a certain beautiful lake:

"The smile of the Great Spirit." — *meaning God!*

"Now we see through a glass, darkly; but then face to face: now I know in part; but then shall I know even as also I am known." — *1 Corinthians 13:12.*

THE TEN MAXIMS OF
COMMERCIAL LAW

10 MAXIMS OF LAW

1. A workman is worthy of his hire.

2. All men are equal under the law.

3. In commerce truth is sovereign.

4. Truth is expressed in the form of an affidavit.

5. An unrebutted affidavit stands as truth in commerce.

6. An unrebutted affidavit becomes judgement in commerce.

7. A matter must be expressed to be resolved.

8. He who leaves the field of battle first loses by default.

9. Sacrifice is the measure of credibility

10. A lien or claim can be satisfied only through rebuttal by counter affidavit point by point, resolution by jury, or payment or performance of the claim.

10 MAXIMS OF LAW

1. *Exodus 20:15; Lev. 19:13; Mat. 10:10; Luke 10:7; II Tim. 2:6.*

2. *God's Law; Natural and Moral law; Exodus 21:23-25; Lev. 24: 17-21; Deut. 1:17, 19:21; Mat. 22:36-40; Luke 10:17; Col. 3:25.*

3. *Exodus 20:16; Ps. 117:2; John 8:32; II Cor. 13:8.*

4. *Lev. 5:4-5; Lev. 6:3-5; Lev. 19:11-13: Num. 30:2; Mat. 5:33; James 5:12.*

5. *1 Pet. 1:25; Heb. 6:13-15.*

6. *Heb. 6:16-17.*

7. *Heb. 4:16; Phil. 4:6; Eph. 6:19-21.*

8. *Book of Job; Mat. 10:22.*

9. *No willingness to sacrifice = no liability, responsibility, authority or measure of conviction; "nothing ventured nothing gained."*

10. *Gen. 2-3; Matthew 4; Revelation.*

More Maxims of Law

1. A payment tendered and refused is paid in full.

2. The Offeror is the tail and the Acceptor is the head.

3. You must go low to be made high.

4. An offer refuse is dishonored.

5. An offer commands a response.

6. Creditors never lose; debtors never win.

7. You must give honor to get honor.

8. He who has the gold pays the debts.

9. No one can be compelled to do the impossible.

10 HJR 192 of 1933 is public policy.

11. A contract is a bond.

12. A bond is a contract.

13. Public policy is an unbeatable contract bond.

14. The created is subject to the creator.

15. The borrower is subject to the lender.

16. The slave is subject to the master.

17. The debtor is subject to the creditor.

18. No controversy can exist in bankruptcy.

19. Creating a controversy is a dishonor.

20. All debts are forgiven in bankrupcy.

21. An offer of legal tender cannot be refused.

22. The refusal of legal tender is a debt discharged.

23. Refusing to accept payment on a debt cancels the debt.

24. The validity of the public debt shall not be questioned. (U.S. Constitution, Amendment 14, Section 4).

25. All debt must be either accepted and discharged or paid with notes.

Amendment XIV

Section 4. The validity of the public debt shall not be questioned. — *U.S. Constitution*

Maine Patriot Books
click on links to Amazon.com

GIVE YOURSELF CREDIT
Money Doesn't Grow On Trees
http://tinyurl.com/39eoywm

FROM DEBT TO PROSPERITY
'Social Credit' Defined
http://tinyurl.com/2vjgqay

MY HOME IS MY CASTLE
Beware Of The Dog
http://tinyurl.com/37wk48v

COMMERCIAL REDEMPTION
The Hidden Truth
http://tinyurl.com/37tdbrf

HARDCORE REDEMPTION-IN-LAW
Commercial Freedom And Release
http://tinyurl.com/2ul4t5e

OIL BENEATH OUR FEET
America's Energy Non-Crisis
http://tinyurl.com/34dhbur

CLIMATEGATE DEBUNKED
Big Brother, Mainstream Media, Cover Ups
http://tinyurl.com/3yjjx6p

MONITIONS OF A MOUNTAIN MAN
Manna, Money, & Me
http://tinyurl.com/377l66n

MAINE STREET MIRACLE
Saving Yourself and America
http://tinyurl.com/38lk966

RECLAIM YOUR SOVEREIGNTY
Take Back Your Christian Name
http://tinyurl.com/392kzqr

UNTOLD HISTORY OF AMERICA
Let The Truth Be Told
http://tinyurl.com/36tkc9q

NEW BEGINNING STUDY COURSE
Connect The Dots And See
http://tinyurl.com/37n8cyj

EPISTLE TO THE AMERICANS I
What you don't know about the "Income Tax"
http://tinyurl.com/3yz8mun

EPISTLE TO THE AMERICANS II
What you don't know about "American History"
http://tinyurl.com/33cawzr

EPISTLE TO THE AMERICANS III
What you don't know about the "Money Issue"
http://tinyurl.com/3az8r7w

drobin@maine-patriot.com

Maine-Patriot.com, 3 Linnell Circle, Brunswick, ME 04011